THE JESUS CHAIR

The Legacy of Frances Blake

Proverbs 3:5 & 6
Frances

Psalm 34:8
G. Hen

Ellen Judy

The Jesus Chair, oil painting by Ellen Judy.
Cover Design by Ted Monnin.

ISBN: 978-1-60458-132-4
Printed in the US by InstantPublisher.com

DEDICATION

This book is lovingly dedicated to my very kind
and patient husband Bill who has encouraged
and enabled me to follow Christ's call on my life even when it
meant the sacrifice of time together and resources.

Bill, you are the cream in my Ashland coffee
and the sugar in my Earl Grey tea.
From Angel's Landing to Montpelier,
Living life together is both challenging and wonderful.

To God be the glory for all that He has done in our lives.
Thank you, my Love.

Ellen

A TRIBUTE

To Cleveland Blake, my man for sixty plus years.

God took a little country boy and a little city girl and brought us together. A young man playing his guitar was drawn into my life. With God by our side, we made the journey through parenting five children. I learned many wonderful lessons from this steadfast, honest man. I thank God for our time together.

To Brenda, our first child, a nurse.

Your dad and I both wanted a little girl, and God truly blessed us with such a precious one. We were always so proud of your achievements, especially your piano playing, and the choice you made to go into nursing. The way you have faced obstacles and have drawn closer to the Lord has set such an example and witness for God to our family. Thank you, Brenda, for all you give to your Mom.

To Beverly Ann, our singing girl.

Another daughter and "Oh"what a delight, a sister for Brenda. This little girl started out in life as a follower, especially after her big sister. Now I see her as a leader — one that people respect and follow. I thank God for your giving spirit, Beverly Ann. God is giving you the desire of your heart.

To Byron, our son, the builder.

God gave you many talents—sports, carpentry, and such a beautiful hand in drawing plans. Now instead of building houses you are building a family; the last of my children to give me another grandchild. I thank God, Byron, for how He has kept you and is speaking into your heart.

To Bonita, our miracle child.

A prodigal who has returned to the Father. From a slave to the world to become a King's child. Bonita, when your mom thinks of you, I'm drawn to Romans 12:1 and 2. You are a living sacrifice, holy and acceptable unto God. You are not conformed to the world anymore, but you have been transformed by the renewing of your mind. I thank God for all that you give to our family.

To Beth Ann, our child fulfilling the prophecy.

A prophecy was spoken when you were in my womb that I would have a girl who would bless me in my old age. The love and commitment you have for our God and your family truly does bless your Mom.

I just want to thank and praise my God who has blessed me with my wonderful family!

Frances

ACKNOWLEDGEMENTS

I wish to thank everyone who contributed to the writing of this book. You, too, sat in the Jesus Chair and heard the truth spoken in love as Frances, led by the Holy Spirit, counseled and exhorted us to discover "Kingdom Living." Thank you for letting me share your stories, too.

Special thanks to Aimee West and to my daughter Anna for reading and editing the manuscript, to Doug and Aimee Decker for offering me a hideaway place to finish the manuscript, to Chaille Brindley, Edward Brindley, Jr., and Pastor Pete for their help and encouragement, to Ted Monnin for his excellent graphic contributions, to all who helped to underwrite this endeavor,

And to Ms. Frances who keeps challenging us all to reach higher and believe for God's best in every circumstance in life, who has shown us how to live the abundant life in Christ.

CONTENTS

PART ONE:
OUR STORY

PART TWO:
EXPRESSIONS FROM THE JESUS CHAIR

PREFACE

We spend a lot of time sitting. Sitting in the car at traffic lights. Sitting at our desks in school. Sitting in the pew in church. Sitting in the lounge chair at the beach. Sitting on the bench in the park. From the highchair to the easy chair, much of life is spent off our feet.

If you go to Frances Blake's house, you'll get a warm southern invitation to come in and have a seat. But the chair she will direct you to is her Jesus Chair. This is a wonderful, high back, upholstered, fairly comfortable chair that sits directly in front of her. Her days are full of phone calls, needlepoint, reading, prayer, and visits from friends who are invited to have a seat.

The Jesus Chair is her reminder of how close He is in everyday life. And every chance she gets, she'll invite friends (and soon- to-be friends if they are strangers when they come to the door) to have a seat in the Jesus Chair.

It's something like sitting in Jesus' lap. She invites people to get as close to the Savior as they can, and then the visiting starts. Conversation soon revolves around the wonderful love of her Savior. More than one person has left that encounter with a new relationship with God. And most people leave with something from the Lord — an encouraging word, an invitation to believe, or the opportunity for hope and healing. And so the stories come from the Jesus Chair. Time spent with Frances is time spent in His presence in His chair.

Let me invite you to have a seat, sit a spell.

Pastor Carter Goolsby
Mechanicsville Christian Center

INTRODUCTION

"HoneyChile, come here and take a look at this stockin' I'm makin' for my grandchile!" Frances showed me an exquisite Christmas stocking stitched for the newest family member. On any given day I would stop by to visit her and find Frances immersed in a new handiwork project for someone she loved: afghans for babies, brides, and friends, wedding invitations in calligraphy, and a legacy of colorful quilts to pass along to her children.

In this book my challenge is to stitch together the fabric pieces of a woman's life, a woman who has profoundly influenced my life for good. Frances Blake has been my spiritual mother and a friend for over twenty years. During times of crisis Frances has helped to point me toward God and His better answer for my life.

"I'm just an ordinary woman," Frances maintains, yet she is one who commands attention: strong and secure in her relationship with God, daily abiding with Christ in His Word, and led by the Holy Spirit. Her journey of faith has been long and at times very difficult from her childhood in Roman Catholicism, through years of raising a family, then caring for her husband Cleveland as he slipped into Alzheimer's and death, to the present day challenges of her own health and the life of the church she loves. She shares freely the lessons that God has taught her along the way with whoever will listen.

If you visit Frances' home, you will see that she knows how to make fine quilts. She also knows how to preserve them so that others will be able to enjoy them for many more years. They display themselves grandly on neatly made beds. No one sits on Frances' quilts!

In contrast, my own first attempt at quilting was a candlewick quilt given to me by my mother-in-law, Ruth. It took me fifteen years to tie every knot in that design. Mary, my young daughter, mercifully joined in to help me finish this project. It brought me joy to see her place stitches on this special fabric with her little hands. Once completed, the quilt adorned our master bed for many years. My family sat on it, lay on it, and managed to get it dirty time and again. Numerous washings caused the fabric to weaken and tear. Finally I replaced it with a discount store imposter and placed it beside the pile of clothes destined for the Goodwill store. And yet I do not want to let go of this piece of fabric and the memories that link me to two special women in my life. Now if I were to make a second quilt, I believe it would be a "crazy" quilt of mismatched pieces and colors, for I am happier with less structure and with patterns that zigzag in wild directions like so many elusive memories.

Like her quilts, Frances' life is filled with pieces, fragments and stories that beg to be sewn together and preserved so that others may benefit. Perhaps her story is a "crazy" quilt of love with memories that zigzag in all directions framed by a border of faith that holds it all in place. It is a living story that continues to grow daily as Frances asks God to "enlarge her territory." It is a story of a precious humbled woman whose chief desire is to glorify God and to see His Kingdom established here on earth.

Come, sit in the Jesus Chair and chat with us awhile. And perhaps while you are visiting, you'll see a piece of God's handiwork that will touch your heart and bring life to your soul.

E.J.

PART ONE:
OUR STORY

TURNING POINT
(Frances)

Busy, busy, busy. I, Frances Blake, was in a rush. I had spent the entire day painting at my son Byron's new house, and now I was nearly late for my hair appointment, a special weekly treat I allowed myself. I hurried out of the door that led into our garage and took a quick step down. Crash! My foot turned and all of me landed at the bottom of the small set of stairs leading down to the cement floor. A piercing pain screamed through my right ankle where a broken bone was pointing in the wrong direction under the skin. I sat there and groaned in pain. My husband Cleveland and a neighbor appeared and propped my foot up on a bucket. Someone called the rescue squad. When the squad arrived, they positioned my leg on a board splint and whisked me off to Richmond Memorial Hospital.

Four days later, I happily returned to my home unaware of the huge adjustments ahead. I was on the threshold of the biggest change to come to my married life. It was October of 1992 when God began to teach me that I needed to surrender all aspects of my life to Him. He led me through a painful process of giving up my rights. Every aspect of home-making that I once was in charge of — my kitchen,

1

our laundry, the grocery shopping and cooking — had to be turned over to Cleveland who was equally unprepared for the new demands upon his life. I no longer was in control and I often reacted with irritation. My daughter Brenda observed my growing frustration and counseled me, "Mother, you have to have more patience with Daddy."

"Cleveland, you went to the wrong drugstore for my medicine," my voice rang out loudly, edged with irritation. Cleveland was hearing-impaired so at times I shouted to him from another room. "Mother," our youngest daughter Beth gently chimed in, "It isn't right for you to speak to Daddy like that." These brave comments from both of my daughters pricked my heart. Later that night in the quietness of my bed I broke before the Lord.

"I am so sorry, Lord.
Please forgive me."

Mercifully, God drew near to me and brought me such comfort. My spirit began to open up to the possibility that God wanted to speak to me. I began to be still and listen. His peace settled over me. "Frances, what you think is so important must be given up for what *I* think is most important. I want you to give yourself to Cleveland more than you have ever done before." I listened to that still inner voice. It was not an audible voice, just a strong impression in my spirit that this was what God wanted. I had no idea how hard it would be to carry out His instructions. God had something big in mind. While my ankle mended, God began a reconstruction of the inward person. He wanted to transform me from a busy, often quick-tongued Martha into a devoted Mary who would sit at His feet and listen to His voice. And one by one God began to lead me to give up my rights.

First I had to resign from my position as head of the Ladies' Ministry at church. I felt inwardly calm as I told the Women's Board and my pastor. However, when I returned to our classes, it was very difficult. I

still wanted to preside. I had to give up my right to be in leadership.

At home there was the laundry. I had always taken pride in my laundry hanging outside to dry on the line in a neat, orderly manner, socks mated, a line of pants, another of shirts. Cleveland's haphazard way of hanging items just as they came out of the washer was more than I could bear. Thankfully the woods surrounding our backyard obscured the view of onlookers. I made "helpful suggestions" to Cleveland about how to do the laundry but soon realized that I needed to surrender this right also. I finally stopped looking out of the back window and began to thank God that I had a husband who was gracious enough to do the laundry. My pride and my right to have an orderly line of clothes on the line were put on God's altar.

I was still able to cook a little, but my patience was tested as Cleveland played hide and seek with kitchen essentials. He tucked common kitchen items back in the wrong places. Grocery shopping was another of his new responsibilities. He never seemed to be able to find the items I had sent him for and often brought home the wrong things. God gently corrected me and showed me what a remarkable man he was that he would go with my list and even try to find everything I had asked for. I relinquished the right to always have things at home the way I preferred.

In time I began to see many good qualities in Cleveland that I had not noticed before: Cleveland showed love, not through flowers and gifts but through acts of service. Whenever anything needed to be done, Cleveland was available for the job. He had a strong faith in God and a love for peace in our home. "Frances and I never had an argument," he would brag. "That's because you always let me have my way!" I countered. "Well, it worked, didn't it?" and a twinkle would light in his eye.

Finally, I saw that I had to surrender my children to God completely. No longer in my motherly way could I have any rights over them. And for a mother, this is perhaps hardest of all.

3

I surrender all.
I surrender all.
All to Thee,
my precious Savior
I surrender all.

Blessing Journal

While a husband desires a peaceful home, a godly woman's heart cries out for her husband to face conflicts openly and lovingly confront her when she is trying to control things. It takes wisdom and responsibility for a man to do this. Usually women will step in otherwise or suffer in silence. If both husband and wife will take time to listen to God, and get His counsel, together they can find God's way and His solution to the challenges before them.

Do you have "rights" that you are claiming that are hindering your relationships with others or with God? Write about them here.

_____

_____

_____

_____

_____

_____

_____

_____

_____

_____

_____

Blessing Journal

RETURN TO HOME
(Frances)

I see myself, a little Catholic girl, walking from our home on Floyd Avenue in Richmond, Virginia to Saint Benedict's Parochial School. Mama let me carry my beloved dolly to school so that I would not miss being at home so much. One day I cried miserably with a toothache. My older brother Fred informed the nuns that I just wanted to "get home to mama." I grew to love the kind nuns who taught me. They thought that I was destined to become a nun. I remember the days of Lent wearing a paper doily on my head as we entered the sanctuary and visited the Stations of the Cross. God's hand was on me even then, but I had no extraordinary childhood experience of God, no Joan-of-Arc revelations. I was just ordinary little Frances Thelma Jones, but I was on the Journey of Life.

It was the nineteen twenties. Streetcars jangled along Belmont Avenue near our new home on Grove Avenue. Mom sent me to the drugstore to get some medicine for Daddy who was sick. I skated home from the store with a bag of medicine and a bottle of milk. My foot hit the curb and I fell on the bottle slashing my palm. Childhood leaves many scars, some visible, some invisible.

Daddy, Bryan Frederick Jones, was a veteran of WW I with prematurely white hair from a wartime gassing. He played the piano by ear and was a pool shark. Daddy said that I "couldn't carry a tune in a tin bucket." Daddy was a great sports lover but he was not an affectionate father. It was mama, Catherine Elizabeth, who held the family together. She was a strong-willed and independent woman always ready to do whatever needed to be done for her family.

In the thirties we moved to Colonial Heights where the twins, Betty Lou and Bobby Lee, were born. I was mama's big helper until I was ten years old when I contracted scarlet fever. Mama often remarked, "You were smart until you had scarlet fever." Her careless comment had a subtle but deep affect on my life as I vowed internally to prove that she was wrong. From then on I often tried to accomplish things to prove to myself and to Mama that I was still a smart and capable person.

During the Depression we returned to Richmond to Marshall Street, and Mama found a job as a tailor. My older sister Catherine dropped out of high school to care for the twins, and I returned to Saint Benedict's School. To ease the burden on our family Mama sent me to live nearby with my Aunt Lulu for a year. Our family faithfully attended Catholic masses and never ventured into a Protestant church. One day Mama was visiting two sick neighbor ladies when she heard a voice through her neighbor's open window from the Baptist church across the street. The message tugged on her heart. The following Sunday she boldly ventured into this new church to hear more. The pastor, a cousin of mama's, had life-giving words to speak. "Give your life to Jesus. Come. Receive His salvation." Mama, a devout Catholic, felt a stirring within her to respond to this personal invitation to know God, and that day she surrendered her life to Christ.

I was in seventh grade when Mama was converted, but I don't remember any special conviction about my own salvation. I just fol-

lowed Mama, and at age thirteen I asked Jesus into my heart with all of the faith that I knew.

In 1936 we moved to Ellerson, now Mechanicsville, and Daddy operated an Esso Station/Convenience Store. Our home was hooked on to the back of the store. I enrolled as a freshman at Battlefield Park High School. The Esso station was a meeting place where the young men could fill their gas tanks and play a game of pool. One young truck farmer, Cleveland Blake, noticed me and found his way into my heart.

Cleveland began to work at Dupont before World War II broke out. In 1940 we married so that Cleveland would not have to go to war. People wrongly suspected that I was pregnant since I was only seventeen and a senior in High School. We moved into two rooms in my Aunt Thelma's Richmond home until our own house on Beattie's Mill Road could be built, a little four-room bungalow with an unfinished bath. Because of the war we had no running water or electricity for four years. But we were happy. I washed on a washboard, drew water from a well, made visits to the outhouse, and read by an oil lamp at night. Cleveland built a garage and smokehouse out back where he could smoke meat. Though he gave up hunting after we married, he still loved to bring home turkeys from local turkey shoots. Brenda, our first child, was born in 1942. I sewed all of the clothes for my expanding family. Cleveland worked hard at his new job at Beattie's Mill grinding corn and never wanted to take time to vacation. I saw how others took family vacations and realized that our family life was going to be different. God had already begun to train me to find contentment when my flesh wanted to grumble.

The children arrived two per decade: Brenda Lee and Beverly Ann in the forties, Byron and Bonita in the fifties. Brenda helped to deliver her little sister Beth Anne in 1964. I tried to be a good mother, keeping them clothed, well-fed, washed behind the ears, and in church. They had what we Southerners call, "a proper upbringing". Music

filled our home as Cleveland played the guitar and harmonica and I sang. Each of the children took piano lessons. On the surface we had a beautiful family, but deep within I felt discontentment and a longing for something more. I simply was not satisfied.

During these early years of our marriage I became quite active in the Baptist Church teaching adult Sunday school classes, leading missions work, and singing in the choir. Though I was busy, something still was missing in my life, so I went to work at the Baptist Book Store. Beautiful, radiant, happy young people often came into the store. I felt that I just had to bring home the *life* that they had found to our young folks at church. As I reached out for more life for our youth, I really was reaching for something for myself.

It was 1972 and I was in crisis, at a turning point in my life. Many days I felt extremely frustrated. I was two people, a godly, esteemed woman at work and at church, and a restless, discontented wife and mother at home where only my children's faces held me together. One day in desperation I went into my bedroom and cried out to the Lord, "Do something! Surely there must be much more." I didn't understand that my dissatisfaction was just what God had allowed so that I would be ready for a tremendous encounter I would soon experience. But first I needed to recognize what my real need was.

"Frances, the wrong person is the head of your home." Ken Hornby's comment jolted me! I had just shared with Ken and Ruth Lucas what my work at the bookstore and church was doing for me, building up my self-esteem and confidence. It was clear to them that I was unaware of the price my family was paying for my sense of well being as Cleveland and my worlds grew further apart. Ken's kind, but bold statement resonated in my spirit.

"Why hasn't anyone told me this before?" My question went unanswered, but my life began to change. A few weeks later I invited them to my home for lunch. We talked about my family and its needs.

Then Ken opened the Bible and read many passages which I do not recall except for one — Acts 19:2, "Have you received the Holy Ghost since you believed?" I knew immediately that I had not.

"I have not," I hollered out, "but I sure would like to!" That's when it happened. Jesus completely baptized me in the Holy Spirit. I felt the actual Presence of God for the first time. We sat at the table until late afternoon praying. Ken and Ruth told me of the many wonderful blessings I had in store by coming into this experience. Ken said that God had opened my spiritual eyes and ears, and that now I would know when God was speaking, and what His instructions were. I couldn't imagine or visualize the extent of this new awakening. I immediately felt a tremendous love and peace come into my very being. I began to continuously praise the Lord. And He began to speak clearly to me.

"Yes, Lord? Give up my work?

*But I love it so much and
it has made me feel so good."*

"Surrender it, Frances."

"But Lord we need the money."

*"Turn your money problems over to Me.
I will take care of them.
I will meet every need that you have."*

"Yes, Lord."

11

I obeyed His voice and the blessings began to come. Twice because of an error in bookkeeping, we discovered that we had more money in our checking account at a crucial time when we needed it. Could that have been orchestrated by God who knew what we would need and when we would need it? Does He use our mistakes for His purposes also? Cleveland was asked to do extra carpentry work, and our bank balance rose higher than ever. As we saw God faithfully meet our needs, our faith grew.

Spiritual blessings overshadowed the material ones. My children wondered what had happened to their *old* mom. This new one was different. God gradually tamed my tongue and my hollering became less and less. I experienced more joy and more patience, a new calmness. Our marriage had a new beginning as I learned to step aside and allow Cleveland to be the head of our home. I found new things in our marriage, a beautiful love for my mate, and a closeness that we had never experienced in our thirty-two years together.

It was 1972, God was moving across the land in a charismatic renewal.

He put it on our hearts to begin a Bible Study in our home. We already had one on Monday nights for the young folks, but now there were so many adults with a hunger to study God's word. A small gathering came together in our home in December that year. Before long there were thirty people attending, and we had to sell the pool table to make room in our basement for the meetings. In June we had a picnic that was climaxed with a tremendous Pentecostal meeting. Nine people received the Baptism of the Holy Spirit including my precious Cleveland. We experienced a little bit more of heaven. I felt like I had come out of years of wandering in the wilderness into the Promised Land of blessing.

Blessing Journal

Kingdom principles: Men crave love and respect from their wives and children. Women love to be treated like they are special. They may protest, but they love to feel like a bride, beloved in their lover's eyes no matter how old they are. "Can you see beyond the diapers, or the wrinkles, my love?" In -*Sacred Marriage* - Gary Thomas suggests that marriage is God's design to make us holy, more than it is his design to make us happy. Frances learned so much from the challenges, even suffering, that marriage brought to her.

Consider one of the challenges that you have had to face in life. How was your life changed? What did you learn that would have lasting value?

_____

_____

_____

_____

_____

_____

_____

_____

_____

_____

_____

_____

_____

_____

_____

_____

BUILDING THE KINGDOM ONE RELATIONSHIP AT A TIME

(Ellen)

*"You must teach what is in accord
with sound doctrine...teach the older women
to be reverent in the way they live, not to be
slanderers, or addicted to much wine, but to
teach what is good. They can train the younger
women to love their husbands, and children, to
be self-controlled and pure, to be busy at home,
to be kind, and to be subject to their husbands,
so that no one will malign the word of God."*
Titus 2:1-5

It seems strange that I, Ellen, do not even remember my first meeting with Frances. It was January, 1986 and my four children and I had just joined my husband Bill in Richmond after a three month separation while I sold our house in Waynesboro, Virginia.

We found a small Cape Cod rental house to squeeze into near Mechanicsville until we could decide upon a permanent home. After settling in for a few days, we opened our home to Jeanie, a teenage daughter of an acquaintance from our former church family. Jeanie had just been released from the Richmond Psychiatric Hospital; and before we moved, her mother had asked us to take her in until an unspecified time when Jeanie could return home. On day two in our new home, the children and I piled into the car to explore our neighborhood. We drove along Shady Grove Road until we saw a church that attracted us and we stopped in. Pastor Goodman welcomed us warmly, gave us a tour, and boasted about their dynamic youth group. "A good place for Jeanie," I tucked that thought away. Frances insists that she met me on that day.

On Sunday we returned to Mechanicsville Christian Center. Frances followed up our first visits with a phone call and eventually an invitation to her home to be a part of a small group meeting there. This warm fellowship of people quickly became a lifeline for me. Emotionally I was drowning with all the adjustments we had had to make in our move, and life with our teenage guest was painfully challenging. In addition, we were in the middle of our first difficult year of home schooling. For the whole month of January the sun refused to shine making every day grayer than the one before. I felt like I was being pulled in ten directions at once while my children were fascinated by the antics of this new guest — boyfriends, nighttime escapes out of the window, school truancy. Bill and I had had no prior experience with teenagers. My energy drained away and depression crept in to take its place.

"Honey Chile, you have taken on too much," Frances gently chided me. "I have seen this happen over and over again. A family takes in a troubled teen and soon there is strife in the family. Let her go to her own home. That's where she needs to be. Your own family must be your primary mission field, Ellen. They are your first priority. If you don't have enough energy left to care for your husband and your own children, then something is seriously wrong."

Frances lovingly suggested that Bill and I had made a mistake, an unwise decision to take this lost child in. I mulled over her advice and prayed. Then God intervened. Jeanie ran away from our home and landed in a halfway house in the city. Now we were certain that we had no control over her; and because of that, she could not return to our home again. Her own family would have to take responsibility for her.

Easter exploded into the gloom of that year, and my heart nearly burst with glorious praise as God delivered me from that circumstance. Moreover, I praised Him for bringing into my life an older woman who had so much more wisdom than I and was willing to share it with a needy child of God. Our hearts were knit together in love.

Years later I found myself once again at Frances' door in crisis. "Come on in, Honey Chile. How are you doin'?" It seemed that her door was always open when I needed to talk to someone. Her home was tidy, warm, and comforting, and her heart was open to me.

"Not so well, Frances. I've just been to see the doctor and I am suffering from depression. He recommends that I get counseling along with medication."

"Medication?" Frances gave me one of her pointed looks. "I don't think you're gonna need that." It was a prophetic word. Then she covered me with prayer. Like many other people who periodically suffer depression, I really did not want to be dependent on a drug to keep me functioning. I had hope that I could get to the roots of the problems that were making my life miserable. After searching carefully for a counselor who had a vibrant faith in Christ, I was able to find one that would work with me without requiring medication *as long as I was willing to go on medication should I need it.* This was the beginning of a wonderful yet difficult time of emotional healing

that God has sustained through many years of joy and sorrow. I am just so thankful for a friend who had the boldness to encourage me to take a risk and trust God for healing.

Frances continued to challenge me to examine my busy and exhausting life style. Why was I ministering in prison in addition to home schooling? Had God called me to do this or was this ministry meeting an unmet need within me for appreciation? What was the motive that was driving me? Ouch! Her questions hit the target so often. How had God given her so much insight into my life? Was it perhaps because she too had walked in these same tired and uncomfortable shoes and had learned her lessons well?

Blessing Journal

Write about one person who has impacted your life for good, encouraging you to take a step of faith or just being a good friend and listener.

_____

_____

_____

_____

_____

_____

_____

_____

_____

_____

_____

_____

A TIME OF CRUSHING

In *Hind's Feet on High Places* the Shepherd King takes a young woman named Much-Afraid to view the long procession of his subjects who were traveling through the desert into the crushing granaries of Egypt to be made into bread, bread that would feed multitudes of starving people in the world.

"Much-Afraid," he said, "all of my servants on their way to the High Places have had to make this detour through the desert. It is called 'The furnace of Egypt, and a horror of great darkness.' Here they have learned many things, which otherwise they would have known nothing about.

Abraham was the first of my servants to come this way...then Joseph, with tears and anguish of heart...looked upon it too and learned the les-

son of the furnace of fire. Since that time an endless succession of my people have come this way. They came to learn the secret of royalty, and now you are here...It is a great privilege... Those who come down to the furnace go on their way afterwards as royal men and women, princes and princesses of the Royal Line."

*"As Much-Afraid watched the women pounding the bread corn with their heavy stones she noticed how long the process took before the fine white powder was finished and ready for use. Then she heard the Shepherd saying, 'I bring my people into Egypt that they, too, may be threshed and ground into the finest powder and may become bread corn for the use of others. But remember, though bread corn is bruised, no one threshes it forever; only until the bruised and broken grain is ready for its highest use."***

The 1990's were a crushing time for Frances, a decade of severe trials and of great rewards with teachings from God that would shape the greater ministry God had ordained for her latter years.

In 1991 her sister Catherine West died suddenly from acute leukemia. In January of the following year "Granny" Cummings, Frances' mother, who had been living with Cleveland and her died. In October of 1992 as stated in the beginning of this book Frances

fell and severely broke her ankle. Then in the following year Frances began to experience recurring pains in her head, and the doctor discovered an aneurysm. In October of 1993 she underwent an eleven-hour surgery while a metal clamp was positioned in her head. God's grace carried her through this surgery without any fear. However, while recuperating back at home, she tripped and fell and suffered a concussion requiring further hospitalization. As her head continued to ache and troubles seemed to come in a whirlwind, Frances began to have doubts about the success of the operation.

"Mother, I believe you are on the verge of depression," her daughter ventured. Frances pondered these words as she listened to a cassette teaching tape that quoted Micah 7:8 "Do not rejoice over me, my enemy; when I fall, I will arise; when I sit in darkness, The Lord will be a light to me."

"Well, I set there and I tell ya I got up and went down the hall and I said, 'There's no way the enemy is going to get this.' I rebuked it in the name of Jesus. I walked down that hallway four times and chased him (a demonic spirit) out of my house. And I haven't had a pain in my head since!"

At that time another scripture from Habakkuk brought her encouragement:

"Though the fig tree may not blossom, nor fruit be on the vines; though the labor of the

olive may fail and fields yield no food...yet I will rejoice in the Lord. I will joy in the God of my salvation. The Lord God is my strength; He will make my feet like hinds' feet and He will make me walk on my high places."

Habakkuk 3:17-19

She fondly remembered one of "her boys", Pete Hohmann, a young science-teacher-turned-pastor, singing this on his dulcimer. "No matter how bad things are we can rejoice," Frances reminded herself. Yet like Job of the Bible, Frances' faith and knowledge of God's mysterious ways would be further tested and refined like gold.

Before long her beloved husband, Cleveland, ten years older than Frances, was diagnosed with Alzheimer's. Frances faced this new crisis squarely and cried out to God asking that He would allow her to live long enough to care for Cleveland. She knew that it would be very difficult for her children to care for him and desired to spare them this burden.

Debbie Harper, another of her spiritual daughters, interviewed Frances about the lessons God taught her during this season of challenging circumstances:

Debbie: What can you tell us about circumstances?

Frances: God has so impressed upon me that he wanted me to let the circumstances work for me not *me* work for them. Now that's a biggie. Because I was in the midst of some very trying circumstances. And I realized that I was a child of the King, and these circumstances that surrounded me...I mean God was using everything to bring me into a closer walk with Him. I found that in the midst of everything that

looked so awful God was bringing me to a place of freedom and abundant life like I've never known. Now I had to continue to come back to that because you can be tested over and over and the circumstances that hit your life are not always pretty, but usually the ones that are the hardest are the ones that can bring the greatest results.

Debbie: I've seen that walked out in your life…

Frances: Gradually God was bringing me into a place of real contentment that I would have never had apart from God, because I was too much involved. But I want to tell you something. The freedom that God was giving me…it's so wonderful even in the midst of things that looked so bad because God was giving me a freedom and taking me out of bondage to people. We can be so much listenin' to what man says and what he thinks we ought to be doing that we don't have time to hear what God is saying. I want to be in the center of God's will — which I *am* — more today than ever…I know people thought I had lost my freedom. I had been so free to go and do…Cleveland never wanted to go anywhere but he still wanted to go to church. And we went to the store and we went to the church, but even in the latter part we stopped going to the store …and the only place we went was church. It was wonderful because I saw God gave me more people here, even though I had to be very careful not to overdo the time. I recognized that in this Cleveland taught me many things, even down to wantin' to go to bed early. I cringed with this. I did not want to do that.

Debbie: You gave up another right.

Frances: But I did it because right away I recognized if I delayed going to bed with him it could get him into a stage of being real ugly. He wasn't the same person. It would upset him.

25

Debbie: You met the physical need there.

Frances: Well I had cable TV that I could look at…I learned so many things through Cleveland. God used him to bring me into a closer walk with Jesus because I *needed* Him everyday. And it was so wonderful. *(Ellen's note: The new intimacy with the Lord was wonderful, not the suffering that both she and Cleveland and the family were experiencing.)* If I didn't do things just right or I had someone here too long, it would keep Cleveland from even eating. He would just sit there and sulk. He was just another person.

Debbie: Did you ever think about placing Cleveland in another home?

Frances: No, because it never entered my mind.

Then in August of 1998 Frances suffered a major heart attack. Their children came into the home to stay with Cleveland. Daily, Cleveland asked for "Mama. When's Mama comin' home?"

Frances: God spared me for Cleveland… He spared my mind. The doctor said that it was a miracle that I had my mind.

During this heart attack Frances had a profound death experience with the Lord.

Frances: I never felt alone because in that heart attack God gave me a gift of His Glory, His Presence, and it was so real… It was like He set in that red chair (the Jesus Chair) and… I'd do my sewing or I'd do my reading…He taught me so much…He also impressed upon me (This is how I hear from the Lord — deep impressions. I don't hear Him actually speak out, but I hear it in my spirit.) He wanted me to recognize in a deep way *who* I am in Christ and He wanted me to

walk in Kingdom Living; to exercise the authority that is ours as the children of the King. And we don't do it. We fall prey to these things (difficult circumstances). I shall never forget one day in the middle of our family room Cleveland was upset, but I came against it *in the name of Jesus*.

Debbie: Just exactly *what* did you come against?

Frances: I came against a demonic spirit that I saw. Now I know that I might be standing alone on some of this, but I believe in my heart that Alzheimer's is a demonic spirit. It showed it so much with me. God had showed me this a way back, and I came against it "in the name of Jesus". I just called out the name of Jesus.

Debbie: Then what happened?

Frances: Cleveland backed into the chair and went to sleep. Now that didn't happen a second time. There were other ways that I had to work it… like going to bed early…It might appear that was a sacrifice, but you know anything that we really feel *is* a sacrifice is *not* a sacrifice. It was my deep love for the Lord. I knew the Lord was saying (to do) this. I had some episodes that I had to call out to the children (for help). I mean profanity and things that we never had in our whole life.

Debbie: I've heard that's common in Alzheimer's.

Frances: He had his sweetest times too. I was seeking God to help me to keep *those* kinds of times…The Lord intervened over and over again. My doctor called me every morning (when Cleveland was in the hospital) and said, "You can't bring him home." So we had to make arrangements …and don't tell *me*…I know God intervened, because on Thursday Dr. Overmeyer called me and said, "Frances, we can't move him today, because he's got a little fever and we'll wait and see about tomorrow. Friday comes and the same thing. I said, "Praise you, God," because it was much more convenient for me. He called on Friday, "We're going through the weekend." Let me tell you…we had prayed that God would release Cleveland, but I was uneasy about myself. I think I might have had a little fear because they told me I had to put him in a nursing home. I just asked Him to release Cleveland because "I don't have money to put him in a nursing home. Please help me, Lord. I want my motives to be right."

And the Lord spoke so clearly in my spirit,

"Frances, do you trust me?"

I said, "Oh, but I do!"

"Have I ever let you down?"

"Oh no, Lord!"

"Well," He said, "Frances, I want to bring your trust to a higher level."

And I went to sleep and I felt a peace that I hadn't had, and that was God. And when Dr. Overmeyer came back on Monday and called me, he said, "Frances, he's taken such a downhill turn that I'll give him two days." That's when we gathered around his bed. He was 87…Dec.19, 2000.

Debbie: It was one of the most beautiful funeral services I've seen — so many men came up…Someone said, "You're not going to be

28

able to continue to let people come up to speak because the police are waiting out there. Tom Woody got up and said, "The police will wait until Frances Blake tells them otherwise." *(Laughter.)*

Frances: For a little ordinary, simple man he had the most beautiful funeral. No king could have had any more celebration. I had that lonely feeling, comin' back to my house alone. I'd never been alone before, and God just seemed to come in such a way. I know today that God is my husband. He's not only my Father God, He's my husband and He has proven it. I had a hard time even settin' at the table because we ate three meals a day together. (Frances was used to seeing Cleveland in his seat.) And one of my children said, "Well, Mother, why don't you sit in Daddy's place?" And it has truly worked.

Just three months after his death, Frances was able to share with Debbie Harper in this interview the insights that the Lord gave to her during this decade of crushing: She could see that the Lord was using her suffering for His Kingdom purposes and that He had plans for her future that were good. God had not finished with Frances. There were greater works to do, and she had more fruit to bear. He had a purpose for her life that would continue until she met Him in Glory.

Frances: The biggest thing of all is to give up your rights to yourself and not to think what's in it for me, but what's in it for the other person. And I see, now that Cleveland has passed on, I can rejoice in the fact that I don't have a thing that I regret. It could have been different. This is what I see from the breakin' [of the foot] to take me out of activity. I would not have been ready for what I had to face with Cleveland. So I see all of that as bringin' me into a place of contentment and being ready to give up the things that meant so much to me, even [if] they were good things...and I gave them up and I

29

received in place the *best* things. It might not look that way to the eye, to the world, even in the church...but I see that it was the greatest time of my life, and right now I'm in the greatest ministry of my life...three months since Cleveland's passed...never have I had so much opportunity...God is bringing ones to me to mentor, and it has been so wonderful. The calling that is on my life right now is to see Christian people begin to live in Kingdom Living and begin to live that abundant life.

Blessing Journal

Looking back on this decade of challenge, Frances can see how God intervened over and over and that His Grace was over their entire situation. She does not think it is necessary for everyone to go through what she experienced to learn the lessons God has taught her. She feels that she can impart these lessons to those who will listen.

Kingdom Principle: God showed Frances that she needed wisdom to live life victoriously. Cleveland's behavior after the diagnosis of Alzheimer's swung between two extremes. He was the meanest and the sweetest that he had ever been in their lives together. God gave Frances wisdom and showed her that she was to "feed" into Cleveland's good behavior so that she could get more of the sweet and less of the mean. If Cleveland became sulky and refused to eat, she learned to just let it go and not try to force him. Frances applies these lessons now to every situation. Look for the good in another person or situation and feed into it. Avoid nursing a critical mindset when people and life situations are not to your liking.

Action in Prayer: When we see a loved one going through an extreme trial, we can intercede for them before God in prayer and speak "grace" to the mountain of difficulty they are facing. When the Israelites needed encouragement to finish the rebuilding of the temple in the face of opposition, God spoke through the prophet Zechariah, "What are you, O great mountain? Before Zerubbabel [God's chosen

servant] you will become a plain; and he will bring forth the top stone with shouts of "Grace, grace to it."

Journal: Are you going through a season of suffering? Do you have a Bible promise to hold onto as you endure? Ask God to give you a word of promise and then extend your faith to believe and act on His promise for you.

_____

_____

_____

_____

_____

_____

_____

_____

_____

_____

_____

_____

_____

_____

_____

_____

_____

FOOTNOTES
* Hannah Hurnard, *Hinds' Feet on High Places*
Wheaton,IL,Tyndale House Publishers Inc., 1975, 85-86.
**Hurnard, *Hinds' Feet on High Places,* 88.

KINGDOM LIVING AND THE ABUNDANT LIFE

Kingdom Living is when…before you make any decision you first think "What is God gonna do? What is Jesus gonna do?"…The ones that are comin' [to sit in the Jesus Chair] are much younger. I've had 'em to come right at my chair and I lead 'em to the Lord. But more, my calling is to help Christians live the abundant life. Help them to see. I feel like I'm in the harvesting time of my life. (Frances' interview with D. Harper. March 2000)

In her journal Frances wrote,

> *"My deeper walk with the Lord began when God brought me back from death through my heart attack…Jesus became a personal Friend to me like I've never known before. He is continuing to show Himself to me and be with me every day. I am so deeply in love with Jesus that*

I want to share Him with everyone. He spoke into my spirit while I was in the hospital...that He wanted me to walk in Kingdom Living... and also to use the authority that was my [mine] as a child of the King of Glory... God is so richly using my pastors and the body [church] at MCC to feed into my heart. The joy of the Lord is my strength. I am so blessed and so thankful to be alive today to see God preparing His Bride [the church] to meet their Bridegroom. My God just gets bigger and bigger."

God has given Frances 60 years of marriage and now several more of singleness to learn more about His ways. She understands the struggles that a married person encounters when he or she begins to pursue a deeper relationship with God and meets recurring road-blocks and distractions along the way. The Apostle Paul counseled the troubled Corinthian church in this way:

"I would like you to be free from concern. An unmarried man is concerned about the Lord's affairs – how he can please the Lord. But a married man is concerned about the affairs of this world – how he can please his wife – and his interests are divided. An unmarried woman...is concerned about the Lord's affairs:

Her aim is to be devoted to the Lord in both body and spirit. But a married woman is concerned about the affairs of this world — how she can please her husband. I am saying this for your own good, not to restrict you, but that you may live in a right way in undivided devotion to the Lord." — 1Corinthians 7:32-35

Now that Frances was a single woman again, she had a new freedom to give the Lord all of her time. As she repeatedly said to me, "All of the *obstacles* to this deeper Life in Christ have been removed from my life." This word "obstacle" was difficult for me to accept in reference to her husband, Cleveland, but Frances explained that in her estimation not all obstacles are necessarily bad. She simply understood and accepted the reality that marriage created demands upon her that now were gone.

But let me share this with you in her own words:

"I'm living in Kingdom living. I'm walking in Kingdom living. I'm free. I'm living an abundant life. All these things because He's taken one obstacle after another out of my way, blessed Cleveland being one of the big ones. Not that all things were bad but that [they] are things that take part of your time. And now my whole time can be spent with the Lord. I don't have to go to bed at a certain time or eat at a certain time. I don't have

those things in my way. I'm not a working person so I don't have to go to work. I don't have little children to have to raise anymore... all of this is taken out of my way...I have an abundant life and God spared my life."

"What is abundant life?" Debby Harper asked Frances.

"When I one hundred percent depend upon Jesus for my all. When I say that, it isn't that I've gotten there, but He's gonna help me... I am so excited when I get up in the morning about just what God is gonna do today, because God shows His favor on me everyday."

"Where...my flesh would cry out...my income has been cut too...I can't tell you how God has helped me to meet every obligation. And if God wants me to stay in this place [she pauses, reflects about her comfortable home that she loves, and considers her words]...my whole desire is to be in the center of God's will...Life is exciting."

It is evident to those who come to her home seeking spiritual refreshment that Frances has discovered within herself a deep well of Spirit Life that energizes her interactions with others. She speaks with an authority that comes from spending much time alone with God. It is her heart's desire to be led by the Spirit of God and not by

her own thoughts, opinions, or limitations. She daily sits before God to attune her spirit to His Spirit. She gains confidence as she hears God's voice and boldly shares His Word with whoever will listen. Ministers, unsuspecting door-to-door salesmen, phone solicitors, a person sitting beside her in the doctor's office — all fall within the scope of her influence.

Frances has several girls that come by her home to help her with cleaning.

*"One of the little cleanin'girls said, 'You're 81 years old? My mother's just in her 60's and you look a whole lot younger than she.' I said, 'That's Jesus! That's Jesus...My body's frail but my spirit is young as it's ever been. So what you see is my spirit...My spirit is gonna rule!' That's what is ruling in my life. That's why **life** is in this house, not death! See, if the body was ruling, it would be so deathly. I wouldn't have people comin' in here like they are. When I'm talking, I want them to see Jesus, because I am experiencing Jesus. And I want them to let the spirit override the body and the soul. Because that's the only way, through faith, that we're gonna be seated with Him in heavenly places."*

"Kingdom Living! Abundant Life!" The words ring like a trumpet call to come up to higher ground. I, Ellen, find myself longing for

more of this life. And before me is an older woman who is visible proof that there is more. I sit at her feet and we pray together.

Blessing Journal

In order to have Kingdom Living, Frances learned that she needed to follow Kingdom Principles. One of the most important principles she learned dealt with the use of our words. God told her to speak words that *edify, strengthen, build up, and restore.* Speak words of Life and not death.

> *Death and Life are in*
> *the power of the tongue."*
> Proverbs 18:21

Why not write a letter or a prayer filled with words of life? Encourage someone else by blessing them with your words of love. Or give the Lord joy today by writing your own psalm of praise to Him.

6

GETTING MY
ROOTS DOWN DEEP

*"I'm a firm believer in getting your roots in.
And I've got my roots in. So therefore, when
my roots are so strong I'm not going to be
swayed with every wind."*

(Frances)

---

*"And he will be like a tree firmly
planted by streams of water,
which yields its fruit in its season."*

(Psalm 1:3)

"Lord, I am thirsty for more of You."

"Then drink deeply from my Word, Ellen."

I, Ellen, was driving west along Shady Grove Road toward Mechanicsville Christian Center when a flowering tree on Earl Clement's property caught my eye. It was a beautiful tree that inclined toward the road, branches bending and waving to passersby. Somewhere hidden below the surface of the ground, there was a root system drinking in the water and minerals that the tree needed to flourish, a root system that stabilized the tree and caused it to remain firmly in place.

"Is that what you mean, Lord?"

"Yes, drink deeply, my daughter."

God must love trees. From the Garden of Eden, to the Cross where the young carpenter died, to the Last Days when two olive trees will stand before the Lord of the earth, God has given trees places of honor in His story. In Psalm 1 He compares the mature believer to a tree firmly planted by streams of water. He communes with God and ponders His Word day and night.

Frances spends her waking hours attentive to the Lord and drinking deeply from His Word. On occasion she gives me a glimpse into the secret, intimate time she shares with Him. Each morning she awakens with expectancy, "Well, Lord, what are you gonna do today?" Sometime after rising, she finds her way to one of the two chairs in her living room where she meets with her Friend Jesus.

"I feel like my devotionals are to have in the mornin'. I feel like I want to look to God in the early hour instead of the late hour. And so I sit in the chair over there…In my devotional, it is always something speaking to me. It's not, 'I wish somebody else could hear that.' It's always a word that God can give to *me*. And then, it just so happens, that everyday I pray the Jabez Prayer because it just happens to be in one of my devotional books. I don't know why, but God

has me looking to the heavens when I say it, and it's like I'm just talkin' to God. 'God bless me!' And I do believe that God wants to bless us all, but He's waiting for us to ask for it."

A Bible is within her easy reach. Small stacks of books and devotionals beside these chairs beckon to her. Names like Andrew Murray, Bill Bright, Anne Graham Lotz, Watchman Nee; these and others have been her personal mentors; meeting a need that Frances had to be discipled.

"I don't remember anybody ever telling me the things that I am telling you, Ellen. When I was younger there didn't seem to be much disciplin' goin' on in the church."

Frequently, Frances takes her Bible and study materials to the kitchen table for a deeper study of the Word:

"When I was privileged…to speak on prayer, I set at this table and it was a delight. It wasn't a burden to me. I was delighted in it — to get into the Word and see what it was talking about prayer. I don't believe we as a whole have known how to pray aright — effectively, and I began to get new revelations on it. It was beautiful! Until I found I wanted to do that more than some other things. I was just sittin' here and I was just gleanin' from it because God began to show me what it means to walk in the spirit. And the things of the Lord are all spirit."

Frances' phone rings — her connection to the Body of Christ throughout the week. It's her prayer partner, Carol Johnston. The two of them share over the phone, praying and worshipping God in unity of spirit. They do this weekly and build one another up sharing passages from devotional books, insights into the Word of God, and personal concerns, and then giving them to God. Frances' roots drink deeply.

God must love trees. Psalm 92:12-14 states "The righteous shall flourish like a palm tree… *They shall still bear fruit in old age*; they shall be fresh and flourishing…" Did God have Frances in mind when

41

He inspired this psalm? "My body may be old but my spirit's as young as it's ever been!" Frances' voice is exuberant. How amazing to see that one can be finishing this life with so much zest!

Blessing Journal

Are your roots deep in the Word of God? Have you found your place in the Body of Christ? Do you have someone to pray with regularly? Share your thoughts here with the One who loves you the most and who knows your every need. Be open and honest and let your concerns come into His Light where they can be seen and touched and acted upon. Please don't hide from the One who knows your name. No one loves you more.

_____

_____

_____

_____

_____

_____

_____

_____

_____

_____

_____

_____

_____

_____

_____

PRUNING

"Every branch that bears fruit,
He prunes it, that it may bear more fruit..."
(John 15:2)

"I've had a lot of pruning in my life and I'm still being pruned. But my roots are in. So when I'm pruned it's bringing forth richer fruit. Now if you don't get your roots down, you'll never have good fruit, because it will be swish, swish, swish... God is looking at the fruit. He's not looking at the gifts, I do believe in my heart." (Frances)

Pruning Day. Quietly I, Ellen, watched the young man climb up the huge tulip poplar tree that dominated our side yard in our home

in Waynesboro. This was a favorite tree of ours, and the children loved to swing on the old-fashioned plank swing hanging from a huge branch. Above this branch loomed another large branch that was diseased and dying and needed to be cut out before the weakened limb broke on its own accord and damaged the rest of the tree, or fell on one of our children. It was only a matter of minutes before the severed branch came crashing dramatically to the ground. After this pruning a sticky black substance was painted over the clean wound in the tree, and the healing process began.

"Hmm," I thought. "This is what pruning is like: a clean cut made quickly, the dead parts removed, and a wound thoroughly covered while the healing process begins. 'Lord, when you prune me, will it be done so quickly?'" The pruning that occurs in our lives is usually not a pleasant time; rather, it is often a time of loss and sorrow. But when God prunes us, it is so that we will bear more fruit for His Kingdom. He has something good in mind for us and for others, too.

Today, Frances and I sip hot tea at her kitchen table. We split a rich banana muffin from Coffee Lane, a favorite shop close by that we both enjoy. Neither of us really needs the muffin, but we happily enjoy some guilt-free pleasure.

"God doesn't prune an unbeliever, Ellen. It is His own children He works upon. But you don't need to worry. You don't have to die like I did," Frances reassures me, "but some things in you *do* have to die."

Yes, Frances, I know: My desires to fix things, to have a picture-perfect life, to control events and the choices of those I love, and my tendency to envy those who have great accomplishments…the list is long. God has already taken his pruning shears to my life numerous times. How many more dead branches will He find? My spirit cries out, "Go ahead, God! Cut it all out!" But my flesh rebels, "No!" I must trust that God will win this recurring battle with my unyielding will. He promises that He will finish the work that He's begun in me. But I know how often I have failed to cooperate with Him.

"Ellen, look at that beautiful dogwood tree in my front yard. It's just amazin' how it was broke off during a violent storm so that only a little bit was left above the ground. And then it grew back...and look at it now! It just reminds me of what God has done in my life...transformation!

"And that's why you've got to have your roots down deep."

Trees, deep roots, and pruning — again these themes run through our conversation. I am reminded of the little magnolia tree in the Judy family front yard that was crushed by a large oak tree that fell during Hurricane Isabel. Its bark was stripped in several places. My husband Bill rescued it with a chainsaw, cutting the larger tree up and moving it away from the young bent and scarred sapling. Then he propped it up with poles, painted tar on the wounded areas, and hoped that it would recover. Now, years later, it looks to me like a large Japanese bonsai tree with a unique shape and a story to tell: *there is Hope.* When the storms and times of pruning come — and I *know* they will — I want my roots to be deep in the soil of God's love and His Word where the underground streams of water will keep me alive. Then after the pruning and the deaths of ideas, hopes, or even loved ones I hold so dear, I trust that I too, like Frances, will bear more fruit for His Kingdom.

Blessing Journal: The Tree of Life

*"A shoot will come up from
the stump of Jesse; from his roots
a Branch will bear fruit."*

(Isaiah 11:1)

This Old Testament verse tells of the coming of the Messiah. Jesus Christ came forth from the family line of Jesse, the father of

King David. He is the Tree of Life. He died so that we too might have Abundant Life. Do you know Him intimately? He longs to call you Friend.

I (Ellen) made a personal decision to receive Jesus Christ as my Savior after reading a Christian book. At the end of the book the author included the sinner's prayer. Though I had been raised in a church, I was spiritually blind and more of a self-focused humanist. I didn't really understand all the religious talk or from what I needed to be saved. Nevertheless, I had felt God's merciful hand on my life and I sensed inwardly that this book was part of His plan for me. So I prayed with the little bit of faith that I had:

"Lord, Jesus, I know that I am a sinner and that I cannot save myself by my good works. I believe that you died for me and that you shed your blood for my sins on the cross. I believe that you rose again from the dead. And now I am receiving you as my personal Savior, my Messiah and Lord, my only hope of salvation. I know that I'm a sinner and deserve God's wrath and judgment. I know that I cannot save myself. Lord, be merciful to me, a sinner, and save me according to the promise of Your Word. I want Christ to come into my heart now to be my Savior, Lord, and Master.

Signed: _____

Date: _____

Perhaps this is your day to come into the family of God. Would you like to pray this prayer with us?

If you are already a believer, have you been pruned? Have you seen God turn your difficult experience into a blessing, a time of suffering into good, your weeping into laughter, and your sorrow into dancing? Sometimes I dance and cry at the same time as God reassures me that He is in control! Hallelujah!

If you have signed the above prayer having taken Christ as your personal Savior and Lord, tell someone else and write to me. Ellen Judy, 15427 South Cedar Creek Lane, Montpelier, VA 23192 or send an email to ellenfjudy@yahoo.com.

FRIENDS

"For I was a stranger and you took me in."
Matthew 25:35b

*"A friend loves at all times and
a brother is born for adversity."*
Proverbs 17:17

Dear Frances,

On this "Appreciation Sunday" there could be none to whom I could write that deserved my wholehearted appreciation more than you. You not only were the cause of my coming to this church when I first began to "know" God, but you have continually been an inspiration to me. Your sincere interest in me from the beginning when I was a stranger to you, made me want to please you, and I realized I could do this by coming to church regularly which led to my finding God. I truly believe God sent you to me.

Since I have known you, you have been working for God and it has made me more unselfish by watching your life and trying to be more like you. Your friendship continues to guide me in the right direction. I only pray that someday I can help someone as much as you have helped me.

Thanks, for being a Christian.

Love, Odean [Smithers]

Frances could have written her own book on friendship evangelism long before the term became popular in church circles. Frances enriched others, by welcoming them into her heart and home, by listening to their stories, and then by sharing Jesus with them. Many in turn became lifelong friends and have blessed Frances in return.

One beloved friend, Shirley Butler, and her husband Henry received the Baptism of the Holy Spirit in Frances' home and within three years they were led to pursue ministerial studies at Oral Roberts University. Shirley and her husband were ushering at Shady Grove United Methodist Church when they first encountered Frances:

"You stood in the pulpit...and sang out 'He Touched Me,' The Spirit of the Living God knit my heart to your heart. Weeks went by before I actually knew your name. I can remember asking, 'Who was that woman?' Then my beloved brother, Bob Bremner, felt the leading of the Lord to invite Henry and me to your home for the Bible Study... When I knew it was the woman who sang, 'He touched Me,' Wild horses could not

50

have kept me away. That first night My Spirit Fire was lit!!! It has never gone out."

The milk and bread that Frances fed these two hungry souls have come back to Frances at significant moments in her life. Shirley walks with a prophetic gifting and Henry preaches the Word of God. (In Part Two of this book you will find Henry's teaching on the "Five Giants," a teaching that Frances has been sharing with the church today.) When Cleveland died, Shirley was one of the first people Frances called. The following is a portion from Shirley's journal:

12/18/00 Today Frances called to say that Cleveland's condition had worsened to a comatose state. He now lays quietly. Doctors say two days at the most before he leaves us. Thanks be to God, no nursing home will be in this picture. A specific answer to Frances' prayer...

12/19/00 5:15am. Phone rings, it's Frances... "Shirley, he's gone." The word keeps flowing over and over in my head... "May it be done unto me according to your word." Coming downstairs to find and read again the passage from Luke. Was it Frances or Mary speaking? What does it mean? In my search, my eyes fell on Luke 2:29, 30...the words of Simeon: "Lord,

now You are letting your servant DEPART IN PEACE, <u>according to your Word</u>. For MY eyes have seen the salvation of the Lord." [Emphasis added] Lord, in times past when an unexpected death occurs, I have heard You say this... "For MY eyes have seen..." I believe when one's eyes really see You in their presence, they don't want to come back to this life. I believe these too were the words of our beloved Cleveland.

Shirley and Henry were friends who were born to be with Frances during this time of adversity. Shirley reflected in her journal about the example that Frances had walked out before them—one who like Mary in the Christmas Story had accepted God's will for her life even though it meant a difficult path:

"I see afresh how my beautiful mentor/role model Frances LEANED INTO the situation that faced her. Instead of allowing division from her husband, she held onto and helped Cleveland in the frailty of his mind. He wanted her (never breaking his vow to her) and she vowed to uphold that. Like Mary, quietly, modestly, submitting to the role now handed to her to walk out BY HER SHEER FAITH IN GOD. No rebellion,

no sympathetic boasting of 'poor me.' But rather allowing the Lord to become Her Husband indeed."

Blessing Journal

"Make new friends, but keep the old. One is silver and the other gold." I (Ellen) loved this song from my Girl Scout Days. Do you remember another helpful saying? "To make a friend, be a friend."

Whether you have many friends or just a few, let today be a day in which you cherish both old and new friends. Why not get in touch with a friend and let them know how much they mean to you? (I just made a phone call!) Or pray for one who has decided to break off relationships with you. Forgive them. Long-lasting friendships require ongoing forgiveness. Or should the opportunity arise, begin a new friendship today. If you need a friend, ask the Lord to send one your way. And while you wait, press into Him for He is "a friend who sticks closer than a brother." (Proverbs 18:24)

THE JESUS CHAIR
AND THE JABEZ PRAYER

"Hey, Frances, it's Carter."

"Come on in, Carter. The door's open."

The young youth pastor let himself in and walked into the living room where Frances was waiting.

"Just set there in the Jesus Chair."

The words tumbled spontaneously out of Frances' mouth. Pastor Carter pulled the old red armchair closer to create a comfortable atmosphere in which they could talk. The red chair now had a name and a destiny.

THE JESUS CHAIR: A Legacy of Frances Blake

When Bruce Wilkerson published *The Jabez Prayer*, Frances began to pray the Jabez Prayer daily, asking God "to bless me and enlarge my territory," to give her more opportunities to speak to others about Jesus and to extend His kingdom. Though most of her energies were focused on caring for her husband and making it through the trials God had permitted, Frances continued to extend hospitality whenever possible to old friends and new church acquaintances. After her time in the purifying fire of a heart attack, Frances discovered that she had a bold message from God to give to others about Kingdom Living and a new and powerful anointing to speak God's word into the lives of those who visited her. After Cleveland's death, stories about the Jesus Chair began to reach the ears of the other pastors at MCC. Pastor Fred Michaux asked each of his staff to pay a visit to Frances and to take a turn sitting in the Jesus Chair. Many of their personal accounts are included in Part Two of this book.

"Enlarge my territory, Lord." Stories about Frances and the Jesus Chair spread into the community. One woman heard about the Jesus Chair while at work in a local school cafeteria and made her way to Frances' door. A few pastors from other churches came and found a listening ear, a comforting Presence, and a word from the Lord to touch their need. During a phone conversation about routine insurance matters, Frances ministered to a woman from Wisconsin. This woman called her back after work asking for spiritual counsel.

"Enlarge my territory, Lord." Frances' ministry went international when a group of Christmas carolers from MCC came into Frances' living room. Among the carolers was a Dheena, young Hindu woman from Sri Lanka, who had made a "deal" with God. For a year she had been waiting for God to reveal Himself to her in a tangible way. If the Christians who were witnessing to her about Jesus were right and she could *see* Him, then she would give her life to Him. That night Jesus met her in a powerful encounter in the Jesus Chair:

"Saturday, December 17th, 2005, I was invited by my very good friend Earleen Coburn to go Christmas caroling with some other friends from MCC. I had seen Christmas caroling on TV but never experienced it and I was honored. My fiancé and daughter came along with me.

"We went from house to house and finally came to the home of Frances Blake. All I knew about her was that she was one of the founders of MCC. I had never met the woman in my life or seen her at MCC, despite the fact that she is there every Sunday. The moment I stepped foot into that house, I knew something was going to happen that night, but I didn't know what. I felt a vibration. I felt weird. I felt uneasy. I wanted to cry for no reason.

"As we entered her house, there she was—Frances, an 82-year-old woman sitting on her easy chair crocheting. My 3-year-old daughter, Sasha, and her friend, Sophia, ran right up to her and sat on her lap directly in front of me. As the group began singing the first song, 'Hark the Herald Angels Sing', I started crying. I don't know why, but tears were rolling down my eyes as if I had lost a loved one. I couldn't sing any of the carols. I felt so uneasy.

"I felt my right hand being pulled out of the pocket of my jacket toward a big red armchair to my right. I felt as if something was telling me that I needed to come and sit on the chair ***immediately!*** I was pouring in sweat and my legs were trembling. Directly in front of me, I saw my daughter staring straight into my eyes. I could swear she never blinked for a second and she had this firm look on her face. I kept blowing her kisses but she never responded. She was so calmly leaning against Frances and staring into my eyes.

"When our caroling ended, Cindy Smith, another friend, started asking Frances questions about her age and her life and about this chair called the 'Jesus Chair'. Frances pointed to the chair. It was the very same chair to which I was being drawn. I was so afraid and again my eyes went to Sasha who was still staring at me. She gave me that look as if she was the mommy and I was the child who had made a mistake.

"Then for no apparent reason, Frances asked if everyone in the room was 'saved'. I wanted to put my hand up and say I wasn't, but I couldn't move my right hand. I felt something holding it down. Suddenly across the room, one of the ladies who knew my 'deal' with God told her that I was not 'saved' yet. Frances got up and asked me why. I didn't know how to explain it so Earleen explained about my 'deal' with God. Then Frances said, "Well, I would hope that you can *see Jesus* in me, and surely you can *see Jesus* in all these people you have been caroling with." Then she said, "and of course you can *see Jesus* in this child," pointing to my daughter who was still sitting comfortably on her lap. That last statement just blew me away. I felt like falling on the ground.

"Frances...asked me if I would like them to pray for me. I said, 'Okay, sure, there is nothing I have to lose. Many people have prayed for me before, so go ahead.' She asked me to sit in the "Jesus Chair."

"It looked like a normal, red living-room arm chair. But when I sat down, it did not feel like I was sitting in a chair. I found myself sitting on a lap – Jesus' lap. It was very warm and I could tell I was sitting on one leg of His lap. The same way Sasha was sitting on Frances' lap. **I was extremely shocked.** I felt His warm legs, and tears just started rolling down my eyes. I tried to lean back, but I felt something pushing me forward as if it was saying 'Sit forward and listen to the prayer.'

"Cindy Smith started praying for me first. I remember the first time she prayed for me a year ago and I told her, 'No, I'm not ready to accept the Holy Spirit.' Now, I was crying so much, all I wanted was a napkin, but nobody offered me one. Cindy said a few words of prayer. I can't recall what she actually said, but one sentence had the word 'sacrifice' in it. That was when I told God, 'You have kept Your part of the bargain. I *feel* You, and I believe in You. That's all I wanted. Now it's my turn to keep my part of the bargain and I surrender my life to You.' That very moment, I had five hands handing me napkins to wipe off my tears. At that point of time, I hadn't actually spoken to anyone that I had **accepted** Christ as my Savior.

"Then Frances walked up to me, and Cindy

asked if she would like to pray for me, and she said 'yes.' Frances held my face up, and started praying in a language I'd never heard of before. Surprisingly, I had a translator (Holy Spirit) whispering in my ears what she was praying, and again, I started to cry. Then Frances began to ask me questions to clarify or proclaim my newfound faith. She asked me things like 'Do you have faith in Jesus?' and I said, 'Yes.' Then she made me say it out loud. She asked me, 'Do you renounce all other spirits that are contrary to Him, and give up your other beliefs?' and I said, 'Yes,' and renounced them.

"When I looked up at Frances, I could see a cross on her forehead. * It was a clear outline of a cross. It had no background color or texture. It was just an outline. Honestly, my first thought was it was just the wrinkles about her forehead. She is 82 after all.

"Then Frances said boldly and enthusiastically, 'Let's all sing again,' so they all began to sing 'Joy to the World.' The two little girls, Sasha and Sophia, who had previously been so sedate, winding down from a long night of caroling, suddenly sprang to life. They began jumping up and down and dancing around the room together and ringing their bells.

"The next evening I came to church for the candlelight service. Afterwards, I saw Frances. I had to get one thing clear that night. I needed to know if it was her wrinkles or was it really a cross on her forehead. It was not wrinkly at all. The outline of that cross was still on her forehead. She took me around asking me to tell everyone what happened to me the night before and I told them that I had received Jesus.

"I learned one important lesson in 2005. God never gives up on you. All

Our Wedding Day
Dheena and Jason Yeary
February 18, 2006

the time we spent waiting and wanting to experience Him will turn out to be a dream come true."

In the summer of 2006 Dawn Custalow attended MCC. Her heart was hungry for a spiritual mentor. One of her friends asked Dawn, "Do you know Ms. Frances? I think she could help you at this time."

"Ms. Frances? You mean, Ms. Blake? I know her." Dawn treasured the memory of her mother's friend, Mrs. Blake, cutting her hair and telling her that she was a beautiful child. These words had fed her young spirit and left a warm, lasting impression on her heart.

"So the summer of 2006, I found myself sitting in 'the Jesus Chair' in Ms. Frances' house. We reminisced about old times, my grandmother, my mother, her children and grandchildren and I told her stories that brought her up to where I was in my life.

"I found a wise and kindred heart with her, as well as a friendship. Her heart has always called me "a beautiful one" from the time I was little and I heard her words singing the same song again, forty-some years later.

"Ms. Frances came into my life when I needed a listening ear. She was and still is one who affirms what God is doing in my life and encourages me along the way. She is the one

who nudges me towards the Spirit's leading in my life. And I must say, she is the only one in my life who has been a spiritual mentor to me. I have longed for one such as this all my life. What a blessing that at her age and mine in my forty's that this desire would come true in my life.

"I left for Europe in August of 2006, as this is my home now, with telephone calls from time to time still connecting me with Ms. Frances. She has a special place in my heart. I recognize the goodness of God in my life in how He brought us together again. I trust there will be many more times of sharing and enjoying together the presence of the One who has made us both beautiful in His eyes. That's the beauty of my time with Ms. Frances."

My own daughter Anna Judy visited Frances while home from Spain and brought her Spanish boyfriend along. Frances welcomed them warmly. "He's mighty handsome, Anna. And he's got such pretty teeth!" Frances tucked them into her heart with prayers of blessing.

"Enlarge my territory, Lord."

The phone rings, a new appointment goes onto her calendar, and Frances looks up and out of her window and continues to pray.

"Mama, you'd better quit praying that prayer!" her daughter Beverly teases.

* This incident in Dheena's salvation experience appears to be what is called a "sign and a wonder." Jesus, his disciples, and the Apostle Paul all were known for the signs, the attesting miracles, that followed their preaching of the Gospel. (Acts 5:12, John 2:11, 11:47, Romans 15:19) The scriptures also warn us about "lying signs and wonders" in the last days that will draw people away from the True Gospel of Jesus Christ. (Mark 13:22, Matthew 24:24) While *believers* are encouraged to seek Christ and His Cross, not signs and wonders, we must never discount it when God chooses to use a miracle sign to bring an *unbeliever* to Christ.

10

PRIORITIES

"Hi Mom," Frances heard her daughter Beth on the phone.

"Hi, darlin'."

"Mom, Timothy wants to show his grandma his new kitty." Momentarily Frances cringed as she imagined unwelcome kitty droppings on her new carpet.

"Well, can he bring it in a box?" she cautiously asked.

Beth sensed her mother's discomfort and wisely responded, "No, I guess we'll leave the kitty at home."

They finished their chat and hung up. But Frances was unsettled and called Beth back.

"Beth, please bring the kitty when you come. It would mean so much to Timothy to share his joy and his kitty with me."

Frances' priorities had changed.

I snuggled into the Jesus Chair and breathed a sigh of relief. It felt good just to sit still and rest, something I rarely gave myself permission to do. Frances heard the tiredness in my voice as we spoke.

"Ellen, are you too busy?" Ouch!

How do I answer a question like that, especially when I love to be active in ministry? All I know is that I am tired again. And the pressure of expectations, my own and others, does not make for inner peace. I am ready to be discipled, to learn from my friend what she has already learned—the importance of having Godly priorities. Perhaps then I can avoid some of the hard consequences that will certainly come my way if I do not learn more about God's ways. I do not want to be ignorant of them. I know that God is for me and not against me, and that He wants me to know His ways for my own benefit, because He loves me.

"Yes, I am too busy." My life feels disorganized, and the pressure is mounting. What needs to change?

"Ellen, you may need to rethink your priorities."

Frances shared with me her own struggles to set right priorities as a wife and parent:

"When you set your priorities, it is God first and then your husband. And church is down

the line. I got it backwards because I let church take a lot of my time. I don't remember ever being taught how our priorities were to be. I don't remember any of that.

"When my kids were comin' up I felt that if I had a home for 'em, three meals a day, took 'em to church, saw that they were clothed properly, and looked after...that they couldn't go wrong. But that is the biggest deception that a mother can have.

"I did the best I knew to do at the time...but if I knew what I know today I feel like I could have spared my children things...I could have been feeding into the good down there as they were little biddies...You pick up what the child leans to. You begin to feed it...to take time with them...It's a responsibility that you've got as a parent that I just thought...Well, I took them to church, I fed them well, I clothed them, and had a warm house. That was training them up...Oh my!

"And you can't beat the kind of love that a child needs...the time, and direct eye-to-eye contact...(I could have even helped Cleveland more, with eye-to-eye contact, because he would have heard me better. I wouldn't have been standing in here hollering at him in there.)"

As Frances ministers to others, the Lord allows her to draw from her own strengths and weaknesses to show them His ways. She hopes that she can help young parents see that *they* are the ones, not the worldly experts or even the church, who are chiefly responsible for the spiritual health of their children.

"If you are not real careful...[the children] can get so involved in so many things that require you to attend to it, that you are not being wise in your responsibility of training them up. And so you are letting the world determine how they are to be trained."

"Ellen, to keep your priorities clear you have to make certain you are seeking to please God, and not man. It is easy to want to try to please people. None of us want for others to think poorly of us." Frances recalls a time when the Lord revealed this to her:

"Even Christians make you feel guilty if you're not doing your job in church...say, I had to miss a meeting...A lot of Christians would say 'Where were you?' God helped me to see, 'Who was I answering to — man or Him?'

"That was when this funeral was for my sister-in-law. I was sick. I'd been sick. And I felt like I had to go to the funeral home for the viewing, which I went on a Friday, and Saturday was the funeral — 11 o'clock in the morning...I was dressed and I was sitting here and the Lord spoke in my spirit, "Who are you trying to please, man or Me?"

I said "God, please forgive me." And I got up right then and I took my clothes off and put on my 'roughies.' I didn't go to the funeral. And more and more this is happening. It doesn't bother me what people think as long as I know it's what God's thinking."

"Ellen, whatever you are doing it needs to be done for the glory of God," Frances shares. "We must let the Holy Spirit reveal this to us in everything."

"It's the same principle. You can have God first and your husband [second] and you can neglect *other* things, and excuse it because you are looking after your husband, but your motives have not been there. You gotta make sure in your spirit that you are doing something for the Lord, for Him, to bring Glory to the Father.

Our life should always bring Glory to the Father."

Take heart, dear friend, learning and keeping Godly priorities is a continuous process that is taught through the instrument of the Holy Spirit who lives within the surrendered heart. It is a lifetime of perfecting by the Master Potter who carefully and skillfully lifts us on to the whirling wheel to shape and to mold us into vessels for His Glory.

Blessing Journal

*"The heart is deceitful above
all things, and desperately
wicked; who can know it?"*

Jeremiah 17:9

The challenge to keep our motives right and our priorities straight is made more difficult by the fact that we often don't know what is prompting our thoughts, feelings, and actions. Life can be so confusing. Sometimes we even convince ourselves that our actions are right, when our motives are mixed and self-serving. I, Ellen, spent over twenty years grasping for what I thought was a Godly goal, a dream that, in actuality, was being propelled in part by an inner desire to gain recognition and approval from others. Only God could reveal this error to me, a motive hidden in my broken and wounded heart.

*"I, the Lord, search the heart,
I test the mind."*

Jeremiah 17:10

God reassures us that He is able to untangle the human heart and guide us with His hand upon us. We only need to ask: "Search me, O God, and know my heart. Try me and know my thoughts; and see if there be any wicked way in me and lead me in the everlasting way." Journaling can often help us untangle our thoughts and feelings about our lives and priorities. Frances loves to journal her prayers. I found the following prayer handwritten in one of her journals, dated February 27, 1979:

"Father, help me to completely give my self to the teaching of the Holy Spirit and to surrender my entire heart to you 'Oh God,' to be ruled by the <u>Word</u>. Help me to obey the Word in everything. And I do believe that the Holy Spirit will give me the grace to obey. May I maintain a walk free from knowingly transgressing your law, Oh God.

"I know that it will not do, it is not possible, to live in sin, and at the same time, by communion with God, to draw down from heaven everything one needs for the life that now is.

"It is my prayer to seek to maintain an upright heart and a good conscience, and therefore, I will not knowingly and habitually indulge in those things which are contrary to the mind of God.

"Again, 'Oh Lord,' I say. May I put my whole

73

heart and life under the rule of the Holy Spirit dwelling in me — teaching me by the Word, and strengthening me by His grace."

This is a dangerous prayer to pray. When it is prayed from the heart, it will bring monumental change into your life. If you are having difficulty getting your priorities in order, perhaps this is the place to start. Why not write your own prayer to God asking for the Holy Spirit to take full control of your life, surrendering to Him to be ruled by His Word?

_____

_____

_____

_____

_____

_____

_____

_____

_____

_____

_____

_____

_____

_____

_____

_____

_____

_____

PRAYER

More and more as I visit Frances I look forward to our times of prayer together. It is sweet to join together and invite the Presence of the Lord into our midst. In prayer He takes us to a new level of intimacy with Him and with each other. He gives us words of encouragement to pray for each other or for the people that are on our hearts. Prayer became the groundwork upon which we worked on this book and grew in our devotion to Christ and to each other.

Prayer opens the doors of Heaven to those who are hungry to see God's glory here on earth. But many of us lack the confidence that we can hear from God and minister truth to others. People wonder how it is that Frances is able to hear so clearly from the Lord and find the confidence to share what she hears. According to Frances there was a time when she didn't hear so clearly, a time when she did not slow down and listen:

"He's always been there but I was always so busy doing, that I didn't get directions clear or I didn't

hear and I didn't see when He was doing something because of being busy. And I think that's a problem today for Christian people. It's the one thing the Enemy uses the most is busyness. I was always a Martha instead of a Mary, always doing, doing, doing."

I have attempted to trace through her life how the Holy Spirit brought adjustments into her life, to bring her to a place of quiet listening to Him, of being still and knowing that He is God. Frances looks back to her heart attack, her "death experience," as a time when she entered into that more intimate relationship with Jesus as her Best Friend. And God gave her a special anointing to speak His word with greater boldness.

"When I had my heart attack, God touched my life in a new way that gave me a Holy boldness to speak...not to be withdrawn or hold up my witness for the Lord. It's just easy for me to talk to anyone about the Lord. It never was before."

A lifetime of seeking God in prayer and Bible study had prepared her heart to be ready for God's new anointing. Of course those who have known Frances for a long time might protest that she's always been a bold and confident woman, even one who enjoyed being in control of the situations in her life. Perhaps that is the reason that she had to go through such an intense breaking process before God could use her to effectively minister His truth in this day. How wonderful it is when the Lord takes a fully surrendered vessel

with all of its imperfections and remakes it into a vessel of Glory.

Because she has learned the value of "listening" prayer, when Frances ministers to others she is able to have a quiet heart and to hear when the Holy Spirit wants to speak a word to another. Often what she hears God speaking is a passage of scripture that she has become familiar with over her years of Bible reading:

"I'm not a scripture learner that I can quote scripture here and there. I don't do it either. But somehow or other when I need it, it just comes up just like that. I know it because I've read it over and over. I haven't memorized it, but I've read it over until it's become a part of my life."

When she was asked to speak about prayer at MCC, Frances compiled a teaching on "Authoritative Prayer" and "Praying In Harmony With God's Will." As she studied God's Word, God gave her new revelations:

"I've been reading about the will of the Father. I'm beginning to see new revelations on what went on in the Garden of Gethsemane. And that when Jesus himself was asking something that could have been of the flesh, because he was man – He became man for us – and he was asking the Father to let this cup pass from him. But quickly...the Lord didn't give him an answer...so when Jesus said, 'Not my will, but

Thy will be done,' that opened us up to pray to the Father in His Will...We have to come into that place of wanting not for anything for ourselves, but for the Glory of the Father. And we have to make sure that when we are praying, it is to bring Glory to the Father. And I'm just hesitating to think that we are aware of this. You follow what I'm saying?

"I want my ongoing life to be one that is walking in the will of the Father. I know that God is a good God and my whole desire is that I can hear Him say 'Well-done.'"

Frances hears people talking and praying about all of their needs and weaknesses and all of the requests that God has not yet answered. She encourages us to begin to have a conversation with God and to include time just to listen for His voice. "Don't let anything come out of your mouth ...begin to have conversation with God where He can talk back to you."

One of Frances' favorite mentors has been Andrew Murray. Frances drank in the truth he shared in his book *On Prayer*. She applied it to the difficulties we often face when trying to make a decision, to know the will of God, or when she is seeking a word to encourage someone else.

"When we wait upon God... When we wait upon the Lord and not run ahead and try to

work it out ourself. When we wait on the Lord, the Lord will never let us down. We'll hear something. He knows our heart. God wants all of our heart and he knows our heart and if we're too hasty with decisions, umm, umm...I feel like I more and more am coming into that place of waiting. Like he gave me that scripture for Carol when I was sittin' on the potty... 'Study to show thy self approved'...

"If it's anything that I can give to anyone that sits in that chair, it is to [be] waitin' on God, it is to [be] hearing from God. [To be] excited that you can talk to God just like we're talkin' and I can ask 'Why God?' I can ask, 'Why am I feeling this, God? Will you help me to see?' And he's gonna do it every time."

Blessing Journal

Take some time to make your Heavenly Father happy. Look up and just listen. Then look within and be still. Let His peace settle and quiet your heart. Wait on the Lord. Listen. Wait. Listen. Read a favorite scripture passage. Listen. In time you **will** hear His voice.

Father, give us ears to hear Your still, small voice of Love. Jesus said, "My sheep hear my voice and they follow me."(John 10:27) My dear friend Rita Baughman helped me to understand why we often miss God's voice even when we are trying hard to listen. Many times we create "spiritual static" with our negative thoughts and

79

words. If I continually say that I cannot hear the voice of God, I block that which I most long for by my unbelief. I must have no doubt that I am His sheep. And <u>He</u> says that I hear His voice. Therefore it must be true. Has God spoken to you? Then write down what He has said. When He knows that we will listen and treasure His words He will give us more.

THE BAPTISM
OF THE HOLY SPIRIT

"Do not leave Jerusalem,
but wait for the gift my Father
has promised, which you
have heard me speak about."

Acts 1:4

"Ellen, there needs to be more teaching on the Baptism of the Holy Spirit."

Today we were going to talk about one of Frances' favorite subjects. I had just heard The District Supervisor of the Assemblies of God say that a large percentage of the people coming into Pentecostal churches today had no knowledge of the doctrine of the Baptism of the Holy Spirit. Frances recalled the day when her relationship with the Holy Spirit took on this new dimension:

"I received the Baptism when Ken Hornby prayed for me in my kitchen. Before that all I knew about was my salvation. I thought the opinions that people held in the church I was in were gospel. That's why when I received the baptism of the Spirit in 1972 I thought I had made the greatest discovery of my life."

Frances had accepted without question the doctrines and traditions of her denomination. But God wanted to show her that He had another gift for her, a gift that He had given the early disciples at Pentecost and a gift that He has given to many believers throughout the church age — especially evident during times of revival. A new wave of revival had spread across the church in America in the 1960's affecting Lutherans, Catholics, Episcopalians, Methodists, Baptists, Brethren, and Disciples of Christ and believers immersed in the counter culture — the Jesus Movement. And the wind of the Spirit was blowing in Richmond and Frances felt its wooing force. After receiving the Baptism of the Holy Spirit, the Word of God became alive to her and she was able to discern truth and error to a greater degree — to begin to separate biblical truth from man's opinions and traditions:

"You're talking about tradition, the things that came forth from the pulpit. I thought opinions were gospel. I hadn't been raised in the deepness of the Word. As we come into the baptism of the Holy Spirit, I think the Word becomes alive...I

mean, the Lord helps us to understand what the Word is saying. More than ever, more than ever, and that's why I think it is so important...it's not just to have the power of the Holy Spirit working in your life, it's God revealing the truth to us. I think through life we are going to have to be dealing with things that are traditional, but it's either we choose that, or we begin to see that that's not the way, the truth, and the life that Jesus wants to give us."

It was a wonderful day when the Lord revealed to her that there was more to living the Christian life than what she had previously known. However, God had to bring Frances to a place of desperation where she was willing to let go of pride and religious traditions and take a risk. She had heard rumors about excesses in Pentecostal churches that were a part of the Holiness movement. But the Holy Spirit steadily drew her. Frances reflected about God's faithfulness to her through her struggles, mistakes, and times of faltering:

"If I've gotten this old and I haven't gotten some insights into some things or some hearin' from God, then what has my life amounted to? If I haven't had struggles, and had to go through some things, makin' mistakes, and haven't learned from them then... I could be the most bitter, the worst woman; you wouldn't dare want

*to be around. But because God is so precious to
me, and God knew my heart, and God knew the
plan he had for me...I am really more and more
fitting into His plan. And for a time I could have
halted it a little bit; even though I feel I could
see God's hand on me from the time I was a little
girl to here now. I doubt seriously where I could
be havin' the Baptism of the Holy Spirit, because
I was very naïve about things that I had seen in
the Holiness movement. And I felt like I had it
all together where I was."*

The Baptism of the Holy Spirit is an introduction into the victorious overcoming life that God desires for us — a life of Kingdom Living — His abundant Life. The apostle Paul wrote "Since we live by the Spirit, let us keep in step with the Spirit."(Galatians 5:25)

"The things of the Lord are all spirit, Ellen. Do you understand what I'm sayin?'"

"Yes, Frances, I think I do." God blessed me with this same gift when my children were very young and I was battling many fears. With the Baptism of the Holy Spirit I experienced an outpouring of God's love in my soul that supernaturally began to drive out fear. It was the beginning of a deeper life in Christ, a life of greater joy and peace, patience and kindness, gentleness, and self-control. Eventually I received a spiritual prayer language that is one of the most powerful tools that I carry in my daily walk with God. It is a gift that I treasure.

Blessing Journal

Many churches have a theology that minimizes or negates this experience or equates it with receiving the Spirit at the moment of Salvation. While it is possible to have this deep filling of the Spirit accompany our salvation experience, generally people refer to their Spirit Baptism as a subsequent event, a time when the believer surrenders more of his life to the control of the Holy Spirit. The believer enters into a more intimate relationship with the third person of the Trinity. Many speak in tongues immediately; for others this external evidence of the Baptism comes later.

The Baptism of the Holy Spirit is a gift of empowerment for service. In Luke 24:49 Jesus told his disciples He was sending them the Promise of His Father. They were to wait in Jerusalem until they were endued with power from on high. Jesus Himself is the Baptizer with the Holy Spirit. What He told his early followers is for all believers in all times. "It is this supernatural power that Jesus uses to fulfill His mission to the world through His church."* Are you hungry for more? Study the scriptures. Read what others have had to say.** Ask your Heavenly Father for His promised gift and then wait with expectancy. He gives good gifts to His children.

**Recommended Reading

• Assemblies of God, "*Our Distinctive Doctrine—The Baptism in the Holy Spirit,*" Springfield, MO., 65802, Gospel Publishing House, 1992

• Bennett, Dennis J., *The Holy Spirit and You,* Plainfield, N.J., Logos International, 1971

• Assemblies of God, *Where We Stand,* Springfield, MO., Gospel Publishing House, 1990

• Dalton, Robert C., *Tongues Like Fire,* Springfield, MO., Gospel Publishing House, 1945

• Hayford, Jack, *Spirit-Filled,* Wheaton, IL., Tyndale, 1987

• Lim, David, *Spiritual Gifts: A Fresh Look,* Springfield, MO., Gospel Publishing House, 1981

• Sanderson, John W., *The Fruit of the Spirit,* Phillipsburg, N.J., Presbyterian and Reformed Publishing Company, 1985

• *p.1436, *The New Spirit-Filled Life Bible,* 2002, Thomas Nelson, Inc.

FAITH EYES TO SEE

At that time Mary got ready and hurried to a town in the hill country of Judea, where she entered Zechariah's home and greeted Elizabeth. When Elizabeth heard Mary's greeting, the baby leaped in her womb, and Elizabeth was filled with the Holy Spirit. In a loud voice she exclaimed, "Blessed are you among women, and blessed is the child you will bear...Blessed is she who has believed that what the Lord has said to her will be accomplished! (Luke 1:39-45)

It was 2003 and God had been giving me, Ellen, dreams about caring for babies, representing something creative that He desired to bring forth in my life. I began to see that, like Mary in the Bible, I

needed an Elizabeth to run to. Once again I ran to Frances. I pulled the red chair over so we could talk more intimately.

"Frances, I had a dream last night. In my dream I was carrying a baby down several flights of stairs to a landing. I placed the baby on the landing and neglected it. It fell down another flight of steps. I rushed down to pick it up and to see if it was all right. It looked fine, but I decided that I needed to take it to an older woman to look at. That's why I'm here, Frances. I believe that you are that woman."

Frances thought a moment and then asked me, "What do you think the baby represents, Ellen?"

"The play I adapted from <u>Pilgrim's Progress.</u> I've neglected it for several years."

"Didn't God give that to you?

"Yes."

"Well, don't you think it is about time that you did something with it? Why don't you take it to Pastor Carter and talk with him about it?" Frances encouraged me to move forward, to finish what God had started in my life nearly nine years earlier.

While Frances had faith in what God wanted to do through me, I lacked it. I was having trouble seeing the value of the gift God had given me and that it was meant for others, and I had begun to doubt that I would ever see a production of this play. But with Frances' encouragement I took the manuscript to Pastor Carter. The church was in a season of severe trial and Pastor Carter in his new role as lead pastor had his hands quite full. The pressing needs of the church demanded his full attention, and the play would have to wait until a Fine Arts pastor was hired. As I waited for three more years, I entertained the idea that perhaps I should go outside the church into the community to produce it. But God sent another dream while I was on a missions trip in El Salvador and I saw myself kneeling with Pastor Carter's hand on my head. I awoke with a strong impression that it was God's plan to produce the play at MCC.

In the Fall of 2004 Frances helped me to teach a women's study group based on Bruce Wilkerson's *The Dream Giver* and the book of *Esther*. We challenged the women to listen for God's voice, to step out of their comfort zones, and to pursue a God-given dream. Each of us would have to confront a wall of fear and giant obstacles along the way, but eventually we would learn to walk with "eyes of faith" and begin to fulfill our destiny in Christ — if we did not turn back.

That same Fall God used Pastor Pete Hohmann to "champion" my own dream and to open doors at the church for the play, now known as "Dangerous Mission". Every step of the way was met with challenges, obstacles, and even heartbreak — the death of my dear friend Kara Benham who had collaborated with me and composed the musical score. But my "faith eyes" grew stronger as God met every need, every challenge. Giants were pushed aside and the play was produced in April of 2006. I became aware that I had finally begun to walk in a calling that was tailor-made for me and blessed with God's anointing. My life goals, so often fragmented in the past, had begun to come into clear focus. Would I have arrived at this breakthrough moment without Frances' help and the encouragement, help, and prayers of many others in the body of Christ? My answer is a resounding "No!" Though God can do anything He desires in my life, He is using me (and others like me) as "object lessons" to the church to demonstrate His overwhelming desire for us, His beautiful Bride, to be knit together in Love as we press on in Kingdom Affairs.

"You've gotta have faith eyes to see."

I visited Frances early in January of 2006 to record a conversation for this book. Frances told me that she had been very sick on New Year's Day, vomiting for several hours. She could discern no cause for this sudden illness unless it had been some food poisoning, but she had felt better after vomiting. The Lord whispered in my spirit that she had been experiencing something *in the spirit* that pertained to the church. I told Frances that I believed that God was saying that MCC would experience a great deliverance that year. God continued to shake the church and many were experiencing despair. Frances began to edify the church by proclaiming, "This is gonna be the best year ever for MCC." In a manner similar to her decade of trials, we too, were going through a season of crushing — God's means of humbling MCC and of preparing us for the challenging days ahead. Would we come through this victoriously? Many were not certain. Frances believed we would. She chose to focus on the things that were good in the church, and she chose to feed into them prayerfully. And she encouraged others to do the same.

May 2, 2007. What are these *faith eyes* seeing now? They are seeing a church where God is moving, awakening His Bride, calling Her to intimacy, prayer, and deeper repentance: a church where God is cleansing, restoring, and delivering His people from bondages; a church where the walls between generations are starting to crumble; a church where children are in revival; a sending church, touching the nations of the world with the gospel of Jesus Christ, and a church filled with younger women and men — Marys, pregnant with God's

purposes who are longing for a Godly woman, an Elizabeth, to be their confidant and encourager and Timothys, who desperately need a spiritual father, a Paul, to challenge them to overcome fears, ignorance, lack of confidence or brash impulsiveness. And we see a church where our Father is calling forth godly mothers and fathers of the faith who will reach out to the younger generations with hospitality and invite them into their hearts and homes to show unconditional love, to listen to their stories, to carefully discern the needs in a broken life, to lovingly point them to Jesus, their Bridegroom King — Seniors who have the time and inclination to PRAY with them and for them — Seniors who have come through fire and water and have found that God is Faithful — Seniors who are joyous finishers in this fight of faith.

"Mama, everybody doesn't have Jesus the way you have Him," Frances' daughter remarked one day.

This may be true. Many of us have days when God seems to be so distant and our lives seem to be put "on hold" but surely it is the Father's heart to bring us all to a place where Jesus can be everything we need or even desire. The time is critical. There is a world of younger ones needing a listening ear and gentle loving encouragement. Will we answer His Call? Will we be vessels He can pour love through? As I enter my senior years, I, for one, am challenged by the life of Frances Blake.

Blessing Journal

What do you dream about? Do you have a vision for something God has called you to do? Or have you allowed your dream to die? It is never too late to serve the Lord or to encourage another to pick up where you have left off. As long as we have breath, we have purpose in life. Write down any dream you have that has God's fingerprints on it.

THE JESUS CHAIR

"Come on in, Honey-Chile!" Frances' voice sang out as I tapped on the porch door. I juggled the tape recorder, Bible, and file I always carried and let myself into her house. Usually we sat down at the kitchen table and talked, but today would be different. Frances was sitting in the living room, and she indicated that I should take a turn in "the Jesus Chair." She had things to talk about that would be off record today, so I dropped my load and settled down into the plain red armchair across the room.

We chatted about my children. Then Frances redirected the conversation towards me and my life and plans for the fall. Was I getting too busy? I had plans to join a Jazzercise class to get my body in better shape, and I would be working at the church one day each week. I shared how I longed to get into an in-depth Bible study so that I could feel more adequate in the Word. I had long felt that this was the weakest area in my growth as a Christian.

"Now wait, Ellen. I think you are missing God's grace in your life." Frances began to pour into me what God had been showing her, gently correcting me as she recounted the truths she knew. She was not a Bible scholar either, but she had God's covenant written on her heart and whenever she needed direction, or a word of God for someone else, the Lord had supplied her with a word. She had been faithful to nurture her spirit in the Word for many decades now through daily devotional times with Jesus and her spirit was alive and strong.

Grace. That was what God spoke to me that day in the Jesus Chair. Grace. God's unmerited favor. I have a Father God who is smiling down on me waiting to embrace me whenever I turn to Him. Grace — that marvelous ingredient that makes Christianity different from every other religion. My "life" bible verse, given to me after my nervous breakdown, was and remains, "My *Grace* is sufficient for you." By God's grace I am who I am. Though I am not a theologian, His word is alive and active in me. And *because* of God's grace I am now privileged to spend several days each month with Frances, often sitting at her feet as we pray together, drinking in truth as we share with each other, laughing, singing, crying, questioning, shouting, sharing confidences, praying and worshiping the King. An empty place within me has been filled like a child nursing at her mother's breast. I am learning to stand and be bolder like my friend Frances — so bold that I even challenge her on occasion. And she listens and takes to heart what I have tried to say, loving me in spite of our different perceptions. I leave her home with a grateful heart, knowing that our time has been well spent. Together we have sat with Jesus, and we have seen glimpses of our Lord.

Frances knows that God has given her a treasure chest filled with spiritual insights, each a beautiful jewel that she takes out and considers, first for herself, and then passes it along to another. She knows that her days are limited; that she has a purpose in this winter season of her life — to pass along the revelations that God is continually pouring into her heart. "To whom much is given, from him much will be required." (Luke 12:48) It is old wine and it is very, very delicious. And so her home has become a sanctuary, a welcome resting

place — for God's spirit, for Frances, and for the others who come.

I am reminded of the last two years of the Apostle Paul's life when he was placed under house arrest in Rome. There he received many seekers and shared with them Words of Life. Even as Frances' outward body grows weaker, her inner man, her spirit grows stronger. She prefers to be at home where her physical needs are met and where Jesus visits her continually. She does not see this circumstance as confining, but as a broad opportunity to reach her world for Christ. Once again God sees her willing heart and is moving mightily in this very special, very ordinary woman who has submitted her life fully into His Hands. Her only desire is that He be glorified and that others learn to do likewise. I think that I can hear God warming up His voice to welcome His beloved daughter home. "Well done, Frances, my good and faithful daughter."

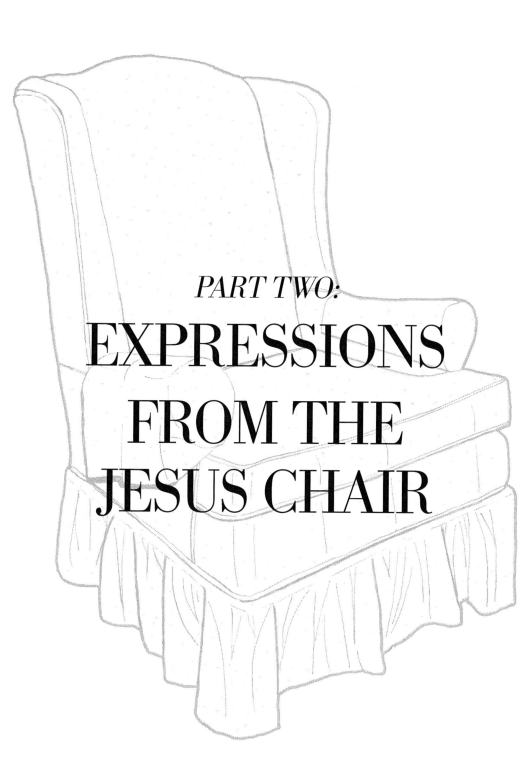

PART TWO:

EXPRESSIONS FROM THE JESUS CHAIR

PREFACE: EXPECTANCY

Expectancy is essential for our encountering the presence of Jesus. The writer of Hebrews says that without faith it is impossible to please God; I think inherent in that statement is the simple truth that without expectancy it is impossible to live in the manifest presence of Jesus.

Do you ever find yourself talking about Jesus like He's not in the room with you? Do you ever find yourself reducing belief in Jesus to a doctrine or theological counterpoint in a religious debate? Do you ever find yourself reflecting on the life of Jesus like He's a person in history who died and all we have of Him is His legacy? Not Miss Frances! She lives every day with the expectancy to know, in a very intimate and personal and real way, His literal presence in every moment of her waking hours. The declaration, "Jesus is alive!" for Miss Frances isn't just a liturgical shout once a year on Easter Sunday. This declaration is the perfect description of her "every day."

Then, as if that's not enough to celebrate this precious gift of a life we have in Miss Frances, she longs for the moments when she has the opportunity to invite others into her reality. She brings them to the Jesus chair so they too might discover His presence, and then giving them the greatest gift of all: The revelation that Jesus leaves with them, remains with them, walks with them, His abiding pres-

ence longing to become the perfect description of their "every day."

The significance of the Jesus Chair isn't just what happens to people when they are at Miss Frances' house. People learn that the same expectancy they have in coming to Miss Frances' house (that Jesus is waiting for them there), is the very expectancy they should have in every moment of their life. Jesus is with us. If you are not sure, still yourself for a moment, close your eyes, gently speak His name...He is with you.

All my love,
Pastor Fred

LETTERS, STORIES,
AND POETRY

A King's Child

From a child's eyes,
Watching my mother with admiration and affection
Wanting to grow up just like my Mama
Of course she could do no wrong
From the eyes of her little girl.
I heard her speak many times of Mrs. Frances Blake,
And the Jesus chair.
Those times always meant so much to her.
I sensed something very special there.
We got to go too, sometimes,
My sisters and I.
We played on the floor or in the grass
While Mama spent time in the Jesus chair.
Yes…something very special.
I knew it was true, but I did not know why.

The faith of a child
Belief even without understanding.

Years passed.
The Lord has brought me through so much already,
Both wonderful and difficult times.
Loving Him has become way more to me now
Than just wanting to "be like Mama."
Now I want to be like Jesus.
You found me at church one day,
After service.
You invited me to come to see you.
My heart smiled.
I came and sat in the Jesus Chair myself this time
And found out
That I was right.
This is something special.

You had invited me into the presence of God.
He is here.
In our conversations,
In our prayers,
In our silence,
In openness and honesty,
In love for one another.

You share with me words of wisdom,
Speak truth to my heart,
Challenge and encourage me.

In the Jesus chair I am reminded who I am,

A King's child.
And my King is the Lord,
And Jesus Christ, my intercessor.
With this status, this identity, this relationship
Comes responsibility
And authority.
Responsibility to use my words
To speak truth, edification, encouragement, restoration;
Because my words hold power.
As a king's child
I must use them to build up and not tear down.

As a King's child I have authority
Over the enemy,
Over circumstances,
Over the flesh.
Yet I must determine to use it.
I must commit to walk in the Spirit
And not in the flesh.
I don't have to submit to circumstances,
But they to me.
Because Christ is my Lord and Ruler of all.

To walk in the Spirit brings freedom
From anxiety and depression,
From bitterness and unforgiveness,
From fear and regret.
Instead...
Embracing repentance, humility, surrender,
Power, strength, confidence,
Love,

Rising above,
Claiming the victory that is already mine.

In the Jesus chair I am convicted and inspired.
You speak truth to me in love
With passion and authority.
You have walked longer and farther than I.
Your words resound true,
Confirmed in my spirit,
Glorifying the Lord.

Mrs. Blake, I love you and I thank you.
Your testimony,
Your example,
Your passion,
Your investment in me,
All have blessed me and molded me.
You are an instrument in the hand of the Lord.
Thank you for letting Him use you.
Thank you for inviting me to sit in the Jesus chair.
Something very special indeed.

Quality time with a quality woman,
Basking together in the presence of the Lord
Seeking His face,
Loving His heart
Together.
You impart excitement and passion,
Challenging me never to underestimate my Lord.
I pray the Jesus chair carry on.
May all who have sat here over the years
Go forth to pass on the love, truth, passion,

and reconciliation
That they have received here.
I being one of them.

By Anna C. Messick
May 11, 2006

Anna Messick

105

Mother Frances

Dear Frances,

Interesting that I met you when I was selling Avon. That was a step out of the boat for me. God used Avon to begin a molding of me that I was so unaware of at the time.

As time passed we were both baptized in the Holy Spirit. Soon MCC was birthed and I began visiting in 1977, and in 1978 God spoke so clear and told me it was time that I moved my church membership to Mechanicsville Christian Center.

Thru the years I would attend classes where you would teach us women how to be Godly women — how we should dress, keep our homes, and how we could be a Godly wife. I still have many of the notes you would hand write for us "girls."

At some point I began to come to visit with you and Cleveland. You were always full of encouragement. Even when your life began to change and you could no longer come and go as you may have wanted, you were still full of joy and always encouraged me to read the word, to listen to Jesus, and most of all to obey what He said.

I do not remember what year the Jesus Chair came into the picture, but I do remember you directing me to come and sit in the "Jesus Chair." As I sat there once more, your joy, excitement, and enthusiasm for Jesus would just fill me and give me the desire to go and continue walking a Godly walk.

Sometimes you would share how God had blessed you with leading someone into the kingdom; sometimes you would just speak truth into me. You would have noticed a behavior in me that was not pleasing to Jesus and He would use you to lovingly discipline me. I so thank you for that. We need Godly women to correct us. Many times we do not "see" or "hear" what we are doing that does not glorify the King of Kings.

One of the things that has spoken to me personally was your prayer — "Lord, let me stay here for my man." So often when life would get difficult I just wanted to give up and just go home to be with Jesus. I did not stop to think what that would mean for my family. I just knew what would be easier for me. Thank you for helping me not to think "selfishly."

The other thing: God wants us to walk in the word He has already given to us. Disobedience is Sin. God is calling us to be Holy as He is Holy.

Thank you so very much, "Mother Frances." I praise our Lord for you and your love.

Love ya,
Carolyn Lantz

Frances in Her Kitchen

Drifting

In 2001, I went to the home of Mrs. Frances Blake in Hanover County as part of a ladies prayer group. In her living room was a chair in which all first time visitors were invited to sit. It wasn't just "any" chair, it was "the" chair…it was the "Jesus" chair. As week after week passed in that chair I had the Word and the love of Jesus poured into and over me as God used Frances and the girls in our group to help me overcome a paralyzing fear of flying. This was particularly important because my mother-in-law, who lives in California, had just been diagnosed with terminal cancer, and we knew we would be taking many trips to the West Coast.

As with any group, the season ended and we all went in different directions, but <u>Ms. Frances never missed an opportunity to invite me to come to see her,</u> which I never accepted. In May 2005, the pastors asked the staff of MCC to go and sit and pray with Ms. Frances because they felt she had a word from God for all of us. On May 26 I went, not because I felt I had anything to share, but in obedience to my pastor.

Ms. Frances would always ask at the beginning of any meeting. "Why do you think you are here?" As I sat in the Jesus Chair I found myself saying that I felt like a boat that was still tied to the dock, but was drifting far out onto the lake. My joy at work was gone and I did not feel like a part of the group at all. Where did those words come from? We talked and prayed together and I left relieved that I had done what I had been asked to do. Aside from that, I really didn't feel any differently than before I came. Little did I know that this was the beginning of God's plan unfolding. Only He knew what I really needed and He was in the process of positioning events that would eventually lead to His purposes in my life being fulfilled.

Ado and I have been saved just over eight years and we are blessed to have had our marriage redeemed by Jesus. But, Life happens to us. We learned early on that being Christian does not shield us from problems and circumstances we would rather not have to endure. I wasn't the only one drifting from the dock. As a couple we had stopped praying or reading scripture together also. We had started picking at each other over trivial stuff that we couldn't even remember the next day. In short, we weren't treating each other like Jesus would want us to. One day Ado remarked that we needed a referee to even have a conversation with each other. A friend at work suggested we talk to Frances. I had no idea that Ado would agree, but at that point, what did I have to lose? To my surprise, he agreed without hesitation. I later came to realize that the Holy Spirit had already prepared both our hearts for this divine appointment.

Our first meeting took place the night of a storm that had knocked the electricity out, so we met by the soft glow of an oil lamp. We believe that this was divine intervention once again. Ado was so nervous that the soft, dim light made it easier to hide. Guess who sat in the Jesus Chair? It wasn't me this time! It took awhile to get the conversation going, but once it started, God just kept giving Ms. Frances word after word for us to meditate on and scriptures to read to reinforce the steps to kingdom living. Some of the things God was saying to us was; to Thank Him for what he is doing and not be preoccupied with what we thought we needed, approach every day with an attitude of cheerful expectancy of what He (God) was going to do that day, to build up and encourage each other, feed our minds continually with daily nuggets from His Word, get prayer partners, and reconcile any broken relationships. We covered many subjects that evening and at the end Ms. Frances asked Ado the question she usually asks in the beginning, "Why do you think you are here?" He pondered the question and then replied, "Before I came, I felt stagnant and now I feel renewed. I see God through you, Frances." Tears of joy streamed down my face. It was like a fresh, cool breeze blew through our marriage in that moment, the kind of breeze that renews and rejuvenates.

Our weekly visits have continued and our relationship is still grow-

109

ing with each other in Christ. We have learned to walk in the truth that we do know and wait with excited anticipation for what God is going to give us. Dynamic positive changes have taken place in our home. My husband has learned God's definition of *Head of Household* and has embraced the position of protecting, correcting and guiding wholeheartedly. More importantly, I have learned the relief and security in letting him do just that. We are praying together and feeding our minds with the right stuff daily. We have acquired prayer partners and discovered where the enemy had twisted truth to kill, steal and destroy our joy. We are standing on the truths God has given us and taking back our joy through the authority given us by Jesus. Galatians 5:16 tells us "Walk in the Spirit, and you will not fulfill the lust of the flesh." We are continuing to try to do that every day because it works.

If Jesus is looking for a remnant to stand with Him in these last days, Ado and I wish to be among that remnant. We can't think of a better place to get our priorities straight than in the Jesus Chair. We thank God for using Ms. Frances and we thank Ms. Frances for cooperating with Him and being our spiritual mother at this time in our lives.

Ado & Lynn
Casagrande
August 17, 2005

Love

Oh that I knew where I might find him!
That I might come even to his seat!

Job 23:2

My son Matthew has a disability that has caused many people to misunderstand both him and us. While I sat in the Jesus Chair, Frances asked me, "Are you feedin' him?" Typically, I didn't "get it" at first, so she used her beloved Cleveland as an analogy. No matter how bad his Alzheimer's got, Frances refused to become discouraged—she continued to feed him with the Word and the Spirit. We were to do the same for Matthew. Clearly, God was using Frances to reach us. We took her advice, and now he's making heartening progress. His doctor, an expert in Matt's condition, has him in a regimen that truly helps him grow and move forward. Matthew is now willing to pray aloud when asked, and even holds his own church services on occasion. Our marriage and family life are benefiting as well.

Frances Blake is love. Everywhere she goes, people want to hug her. Every second or third word she speaks is about love. Her love and faith in Christ are so incredibly powerful that He has used them to transform an ordinary piece of living room furniture into an agent of His power. Thank you, God, for Frances Blake—and the chair you've loaned her.

John Kukuvka

What I Learned in the Jesus Chair

I didn't really learn anything *new*, but God let me see things in a new light which is that it's important to carry myself in a way that is pleasing to God. I was also shown that it is important to be careful with the words I choose with people in everyday life. They can be uplifting or can destroy. Words are very powerful, more than we realize. I want people to see God's fruit in my life. People are watching even when I don't know it.

I also learned that I am a child of God, and I need to live like that. God does not give me a spirit of fear! I have authority in God's name. I should not be afraid of anything, good or bad.

Jesus truly loves us and wants the best for us. He wants an intimate relationship with me.

He wants to spend time with me because I'm his child. That was a powerful concept for me to grasp, but I know it's the truth.

Cindy Henderson

A family portrait:
Catherine, Fred, and Frances Jones

A Beautiful One

I met Ms. Frances, or I should say she met me, when I was just a babe in arms. My mother, as well as my grandmother used to have their hair cut by Ms. Frances, (Mrs. Blake) as we knew her. And, when I became older, she would cut my hair too.

I remember Mrs. Blake being a very loving person. There are vague images of being in her home salon but I do remember that she used to tell my mother as well as me how beautiful I was. After about the age of six, I don't remember Mrs. Blake cutting my hair any more. It would be years before I would see her again.

That time came later in life at MCC when I was in my 20's. I remember being somewhat surprised thinking, "Wow, I can't believe Ms. Blake would go to a church like this." This was a church where I knew one of the staff members — Carter Goolsby.

Years passed and I saw Mrs. Blake again at MCC and we would have an opportunity to talk this time. It was the summer of 2004 and my son and I were spending June-August with my mother in Mechanicsville and attending MCC. I found out that Mr. Blake had died the same year as my father had in 2001, my mother having seen Mrs. Blake at a gathering at the funeral home for people who had lost family members that year.

It was the summer of 2006 though that finally brought our lives together in a deeper way. My son and I were again visiting my mother and again, we were attending MCC. I was beginning to feel like this was my church away from home. Having reconnected with Carter Goolsby, who by now was the head pastor of MCC, and having shared my story with the congregation one Sunday during the summer of 2005, I felt that this summer (2006) I would try to get to know more people there as I was desiring to have a mentor/spiritual leader in my life for the time period while I was home in VA.

I had been talking with someone at MCC about the possibility of getting me in touch with someone in the church to pray with when they asked me, "Do you know Ms. Frances? I think she could help you at this time." I thought, "Ms. Frances? You mean, Ms. Blake? I know her."

I had heard how Ms. Frances was a great help to many at MCC — she was a living legend. When I called her and asked her if we could get together, she greeted my question as if I were inviting her to an old family reunion. She warmly invited me into her home telling me, "You can call me Ms. Frances."

So the summer of 2006, I found myself sitting in "the Jesus chair" in Ms. Frances' house. We reminisced about old times, my grandmother, my mother, her children and grandchildren and I told her stories that brought her up to where I was in my life.

I found a wise and kindred heart with her, as well as a friendship. Her heart has always called me "a beautiful one" from the time I was little and I heard her words singing the same song again, forty-some years later.

Ms. Frances came into my life when I needed a listening ear. She was and still is one who affirms what God is doing in my life and encourages me along the way. She is the one who nudges me towards the Spirit's leading in my life. And I must say, she in the only one in my life who has been a spiritual mentor to me. I have longed for one such as this all my life. What a blessing that at her age and mine in my forty's that this desire would come true in my life.

The summer was full of talks, tears, laughs, and prayers together. Her sharing with me the difficult times of Alzheimer's with her late husband was truly encouraging to me as I walk through this time period in my life with my mother having had a stroke.

I left for Europe in August of 2006, as this is my home now, with telephone calls from time to time still connecting me with Ms. Frances. She has a special place in my heart. I recognize the goodness of God in my life in how He brought us together again. I trust

114

there will be many more times of sharing and enjoying together the presence of the One who has made us both beautiful in His eyes. That's the beauty of my time with Ms. Frances.

Written by Dawn Custalow
Prague, Czech Republic

One of Her Quilts

The Journey

It's all about the journey. While it is vitally important what our destination is, it is all about the journey and living in the moment. Precious to us are the sojourners the Lord puts into our lives to walk out the journey with us.

One of those sojourners in my life has been a dear sister named Frances Blake. Our journey together started during the Charismatic Movement that was born out of the Jesus Movement which started in the early 1970's. Those were exciting days when Christians in denominational churches were discovering the person and infilling of the Holy Spirit like the early church did on the Day of Pentecost.

Frances and I became acquainted through the Full Gospel Businessmen's Fellowship monthly breakfast meetings. Out of that experience, many of us felt the need for more fellowship and teaching, so a Bible study was started in the basement of Frances and Cleveland Blake's home on Elliott Drive in Mechanicsville. That Bible study was attended by a group of hungry, excited, on-fire believers. Twenty-three individuals, including many from Frances' Bible study, had discovered a need to start a Pentecostal church in Mechanicsville. This vision and dream from the Lord became a reality when Mechanicsville Christian Center was started on a piece of property on Shady Grove Road next door to the home of Earl and Iva Clements who had prayed God would use that property for His Kingdom.

From the very beginning, the heartbeat of this new church was missions, table fellowship, and a love for God and others. This small beginning has grown into a solid Assemblies of God fellowship that is touching thousands of lives with the Gospel here and abroad. If there was an MCC Hall of Faith, Frances would be at the top of the list. This Godly woman had set her face like a flint towards God and His Kingdom. While her final destination is heaven, this woman has faithfully walked out her journey, enduring trials and tribulations,

with integrity and honor.

Frances is a strong believer with no room for compromise. She is always available for others to seek her counsel which is infused with wisdom from her life experience, her knowledge of God's Word, and especially her personal and intimate relationship with Jesus Christ. You will not find a more devoted follower of Christ who is getting older in years, but remains youthful and vibrant in spirit.

Frances often shares that everything for us as believers begins at The Cross. That would include our journey which the Bible calls "the race." Frances, who is such a faithful sojourner for those of us who call her "Sister," would remind us of this scripture from Hebrews 12 which says, "Wherefore seeing we also are compassed about with so great a cloud of witnesses, let us lay aside every weight, and the sin which doth so easily beset us, and let us run with patience the race that is set before us,

" 2Looking unto Jesus the author and finisher of our faith; who for the joy that was set before him endured the cross, despising the shame, and is set down at the right hand of the throne of God.

" 3For consider him that endured such contradiction of sinners against himself, lest ye be wearied and faint in your minds."

Thank you, Frances, for being a strong and faithful friend to so many who have been introduced to their Savior through your witness, and for those of us who have been encouraged to keep on keeping on by your shining example.

Your grateful sister in Christ,
Gwen Mansini

Completely Changed

I would say that my life completely changed in the Jesus Chair. I had been praying that the Lord would raise up an older Godly woman to mentor me. Ms. Frances had approached me on several occasions wanting me to come and sit in the Jesus Chair. I kept telling her I would, but never did. Finally one Sunday morning Ms. Frances came to me and said that she was related to me. Her mother had told her that if she ever met anyone with the last name Holzbach that we would be related. God used that to catch my attention. My family had been so divided. I wanted to know anyone that could have been related to me. I started going to Ms. Frances back in 2003 and as soon as I crossed the threshold of her home I experienced a peace and a safety I had never experienced before. Our visits became very frequent because of all of the trials I had going on in my life at that time. I do have to say that I had told Ms. Frances many times that I would not be coming back after some extremely intense visits. But the Lord kept bringing me back by letting me know that it was truth I was receiving through the Word of God and through God's anointing on Ms. Frances.

God had taught me through Ms. Frances that I had to ask Him to help me to lay down my rights. I would have to be teachable so that I could receive what God had for me to learn at that time and forever. I had been so used to doing things my way and to wanting control over everything. God wanted me to realize I no longer had to live that old life anymore and that I was not going to get my way through being the victim and manipulating everyone and everything any longer. As soon as I truthfully received this, I started on my road to restoration and redemption. I continued to visit Ms. Frances. God created a bond between us that ran so deep that we have been constantly in touch with each other ever since. God even had us meet with several ladies that had gone through similar backgrounds as

mine. He used all of it to encourage and bring hope to each one. Ms. Frances has such Godly wisdom that she has so graciously shared with me that we still say that she is my "Paul" and I am her "Timothea." What an unspeakable blessing it has been to have been chosen to sit in the Jesus Chair. I will cherish that time for my remaining days on earth. I love Ms. Frances and I thank her for the many hours of labor she has given me. I thank God for her. To God be all the glory.

Robin Hickman

Wedding Day - October 12, 1940

A Wonderful Oasis

When I moved to Richmond in 1999, I left my dear mentor in Annapolis, MD. I was crying out to God on a trip back from Annapolis in 2001 begging Him to provide a mentor for me at MCC. I longed for the spiritual guidance and accountability that I was missing. I had shared this desire with a friend on staff at MCC and, when I arrived home from that trip there was a message from her on my answering machine, telling me she had someone in mind to fill this role. Talk about answered prayer! She connected me with Miss Frances, and the adventure as one of Miss Frances' "girls" began. I was part of a small prayer group and a Bible study at Miss Frances' house. When we "girls" eventually went our separate ways, I continued to visit with Miss Frances from time to time, always sitting in the Jesus Chair.

I stopped coming to see Miss Frances for a while, because her time was so much in demand. I felt I should remove myself from her schedule to make room for a number of other women who were in desperate need of her help, but I greatly missed my time in the Jesus Chair. In February of 2005, I found myself in a time of questioning. I knew I needed to get back in the Jesus Chair, and Frances welcomed me with open arms. I walked in the door depressed and doubting a decision I had made, second-guessing what I thought I had heard from God. I left lifted up, encouraged that I had heard from God and was doing what He had called me to do. I was filled with joy. I was so changed that I was actually radiant. That's what sitting in the Jesus Chair is all about!

Coming into Miss Frances' house is like entering a wonderful oasis, separated from the cares and noise and busyness of the world. I am immediately able to park all my responsibilities at the door. I sink into the Jesus Chair, ready to receive what the LORD has for me. I see Jesus in Frances. I hear from Jesus in the Jesus Chair. The

Holy Spirit speaks through Frances, and I know what I am hearing is Truth straight from God! Sometimes what I hear is encouraging and edifying and fun/wonderful to hear. Sometimes it is interesting and thought provoking. Sometimes it is challenging and correcting and convicting. But whatever form it takes, it is Truth. There is no doubt about it. The LORD uses Frances to speak Truth into my life.

What have I learned in the Jesus Chair? It would take a whole book just to answer what I have received personally, but here are a few tidbits. I have learned that God has purposes for us our whole lives. Just look at Frances and you see a godly woman in her 80's who is being used to point people to Christ each and every day. This is such an inspiration and encouragement to me, knowing that He can continue to use me to glorify Him no matter how old I become!

I have been reminded a number of times (because I have needed this reminder) that God has given me the keys to the Kingdom, but I have to pick up those keys and use them. It takes my cooperation to be able to walk in "Kingdom Living." I am a child of The King! I want to live like I know it!

I have been told (again on a number of occasions) to make my circumstances work for me instead of working for my circumstances, to focus on God's greatness, and to have faith in the love of God. This turns discouragement into joy. This is TRUTH, and it is easy to believe it, because I see Miss Frances living it.

Frances ends these precious times in the Jesus Chair with suggested Scripture reading, and we always spend some sweet time in prayer. I leave knowing that I have been sitting in the presence of my LORD and Savior and that He has spoken to me through Frances. What sweeter gift could He have given me than my dear mentor, prayer warrior, friend, and surrogate Mom? Thank you, Jesus!

Carolyn Clark

I Accepted Jesus

Dear Frances,

I just wanted you to know how much I appreciated your leading me to Jesus twenty-seven years ago. That was a wonderful day. You and Cleveland came to our house. And we were finished eating. You asked me if I wanted to accept Jesus into my heart. I kept telling you that I wasn't ready. You told me that there wasn't anything to get ready, that Jesus would accept me just the way I am. So, that evening I accepted Jesus into my heart. I want to thank you for being obedient to Jesus. I may have been lost forever. Also I want you to know that there will always be a special place in my heart for you.

Thanks again.

Love in Christ,
Dave White
October 5 2006

In the Jesus Chair

A Legacy of Spirit and Heart

When I think of my relationship with Frances Blake so many things come to mind. She is an amazing witness to the love and grace of Jesus Christ. The scripture passage that comes to mind is found in Luke 4:18 "The Spirit of the Lord is upon me…the Lord has anointed me to preach Good News…" When I think of Frances, I think of a person with singular, Spirit-fired passion for sharing the Good News of Jesus Christ with anyone and everyone. I know of no other person who so richly embodies the gifts of the Spirit: to come alongside another, to journey with them, and to guide them in the way of the Christ.

One of the more indelible experiences I've shared with Frances is an experience shared by many — that of sitting in the "Jesus Chair" and sharing in holy conversation with a person who walks far more closely than most with Jesus. Of the many gifts Frances has given me, one of the most precious is the gift of her authenticity. Frances is one of the most genuine and loving people I know and her willingness to share in conversation and prayer is simply unmatched. She is always available and always willing to share words of grace and guidance. She is an honest, open and faithful witness to the whisper of the Spirit in her life. I have long had the sense that when Frances spoke I was very close to the actual voice and words of God. She is a woman who lives a deep and committed prayer life and her conversation clearly reflects the walk she shares with God.

Even with the amazing communications technologies available to us — cell phones, text messaging, instant messaging, and the Internet but for a few examples — it is still a rare and wonderful gift to share deeply in Christian conversation and prayer.

Frances Blake's witness is rich, and I am, as are all who know her, truly blessed by our friendship and our shared journey of service to Christ. I am honored to call her a friend and I hope that we might more faithfully live out her witness of prayer and compassion for the people of God. I imagine sometimes a community in which we are willing to journey with one another as Frances does with so many people. She gives selflessly of herself, her time, and her heart, ever willing to share God's word and wisdom. Truly, the Spirit of God has anointed her to preach Good News, and we are richly blessed for her faithfulness in this wonderful ministry among the people of God.

Kerry Boggs
Pastor, Mechanicsville United Methodist Church

Frances and Cleveland

My Nana

I know what others know about Mrs. Frances Blake. They know she was one of the charter members of Mechanicsville Christian Center. They have heard the story of her dying and coming back to life only to be bolder with her walk with God. They know she loves it when people "come by for a visit." And a lot of people have heard of her Jesus chair. All these things are true about Miss Frances, but to me she is just Nana.

As a little girl my memories of my Nana are quite simple. They are memories of Christmas gatherings at her house with all her children and my cousins; of playing with the cool Coke machine in the basement from Papa's old Esso station. Nana once did hair from her home so as a little girl I remember the cool hair dressing station where she would let me "do" my doll's hair, and of course I was subjected to perms at an early age! There are memories of going into the kitchen KNOWING that when I opened that avocado-colored Tupperware container there was always going to be Nutter Butter cookies there for us. There are all the homemade gifts from Nana too....the quilts and sweaters for me and Kristi, the cross-stitch works she has done, the baby blankets she has made, the smocked dresses, and most importantly the ceramic lamps that everyone in the family seemed to have....the Sea Captain lamp shows up a lot! You could always count on pulling up to a MCC softball game and seeing Nana's car pulled right up to the fence on the first base line watching her team play and Papa coaching!

These are just some of my memories of my Nana but most importantly, from a very early age, I always knew Nana had a close relationship with Jesus. She didn't have to sit me down and tell me...I didn't have to hear about it from other people...I didn't have to read about it in a book...it wasn't even about seeing her in church on Sundays. I just knew. I've always known. It is the way she lived her life, and for a small child, her granddaughter, to be able to sense that at such a young age means the world. She passed that way of living onto my mother, Beverly Beck, and so this is what I have been able to experience all my life. To have such strong women in my life has been priceless to me. It is the way they lived their lives, loving the Lord unconditionally, that has influenced me to love like that…to trust like that…building my own relationship with Jesus. So, no matter how many handmade gifts are in my house from my Nana, the gift I cherish most is the way she lives her life for God…Thank-you Nana!

Lori Beck-Stephens
Granddaughter

The Cleveland Blake Family

Legacy

To all who read the legacy of Mrs. Frances Blake — you will want to know her. She is a gift given to Christians from the Lord.

The Jesus Chair is a normal red chair with a high back and printed pattern. It sits in Miss Frances' living room directly across from her "sewing" chair.

When folks come to visit they are invited to sit in the "Jesus" chair and from there the Holy Spirit takes over!

Dee and I experienced that on more than one occasion. We would go to visit Miss Frances simply because we loved her (and Dee always said she was his second Mom). One of us or both of us throughout the visit would sit in the "Jesus" chair. When we sat in the chair, it was as if we were telling Jesus — "OK, I'm ready for whatever You have for me." I liken it to a place of sweet surrender. We have found healing, total and complete forgiveness, and a strong realization that God truly loves us and is looking at the greater good on our behalf.

Her ministry is so simple, but so profound. You love Jesus, talk to Jesus, and obey what He tells you! If we, as Christians, can walk that out (or better yet live it by demonstrating those acts 24-7), we too can have a Jesus chair in our hearts. Thank you, Miss Frances.

Patty Edds

Prayer Partners

My Dear Precious Frances,

As you know we have been friends for many years, but I believe the past few years our relationship has grown sweeter and sweeter. The Lord has blessed my life abundantly through you as I witness His love, power, and faithfulness walked out through your life.

I am so thankful to the Lord for allowing us to be prayer partners and causing our spirits to become one, as we go before God to worship Him and to seek His face on behalf of the needs of others; and our own.

Frances, I can't think of a time when either talking to you on the phone or in person that you haven't always made me feel so loved and special. Thank you for sharing God's word and your daily devotions with me so often. God's presence is always so precious during these times.

I believe with all my heart that God raised you up for such a time as this just as He did Esther in the Bible, with the same purpose of setting His people free. He is using the "Jesus Chair" to bring liberty to the captives and to open blind eyes and deaf ears for His glory.

If I were asked to describe you, without hesitation I would say, "Frances is a woman that loves her God with all her heart, soul, mind, and strength."

I love you and I thank you for loving me,

Carol Johnston

My Nana

My Nana is filled with an amazing amount of spiritual wisdom. Over the years friends and family have visited her home to seek her advice and counsel, including me. For those who know me, I am a bit reserved and oftentimes a man of few words. When it comes to my Nana, sometimes a few words are all it takes for us to communicate and understand exactly what the other one is feeling. We can speak a few sentences, shake our heads, and know that each other understands. The simplicity of our relationship is what I treasure most about my Nana. She always knows my heart, and I have always known who lives in hers.

David Bremner
Grandson

Frances and Cleveland - 1999

Happy Birthday!

Dear Nana,

Happy Birthday! You are very special to me. I still remember those days when we would play the matching game. We have some very special memories together. I'm sorry I can't be at your party. It's opening day of gun season, and I'm going to be hunting at our club. You are a great nana.

Hope you have a very special 80th birthday.

Kendell Mitten
Age 12

Out of the Mouth of Babes

A Proverb: "When our heart is off, it is an old season. When our heart is on, it is a new season."

And a prayer: "Lord, if it is Nana's time to go, give us peace about it."

Micah Mitten
First grade

This Little Red Chair

The Jesus Chair is a story about a particular simple red chair that has been the home of many miracles, hours of counseling and encouragement, and a place of comfort and upbuilding for the Body of Christ. To be honest, my thoughts are more about the owner of the chair who lives in a rural home covered with red-stained siding (which she says represents the Blood of Jesus), my sister, friend, and spiritual Mom, Frances Blake, now 83 years in this world.

Frances and the Jesus Chair represent a safe place to reflect, a place to bounce off ideas and dreams, a place to receive insight from the Word of God, a place to receive counsel, and a place of partnership in prayer. It is a comfortable place to listen to an older woman who has gone before us into the heart of the Father. She has an understanding of what it means to be living in God's Kingdom victoriously and to overcome obstacles both in the natural and spiritual realms. It is a place where many tears have flowed, where concerns have been voiced, where burdens have been shared, and where joy has doubled. I have received warnings, wisdom, and wonderful counsel in this chair.

I have witnessed another's personal salvation in the Jesus Chair when the awesome presence of God filled up the room and a soul was ushered into the Kingdom. In fact, I think you could name it "the Shepherd's Chair." At times I have felt that we were sitting in the throne room of the King as we lay bare our hearts before God and before one another. It could then be called "The Prayer Chair." Sometimes it becomes an "Emergency Room Chair" for failing marriages and relationships. Other times this chair becomes a "Gate For Understanding Truth," like the elders in the Old Testament times who would station themselves at the gates of the city to render an interpretation, opinion, or judgment about a verse of the Scripture, a matter of law or principle. Frances and I have discussed many Scriptures in this chair. We have worshipped as we listened to CD's together or watched a video of the Gaithers in concert. Sometimes we just fellowship watching her Atlanta Braves overcome their opponents. This chair is a place of rest from the hurry and scurry of the day. As Frances has had to learn to rest, she can teach others how to do the same from this little red chair.

Submitted with love,
Cindy Smith

"Trust in the Lord with all your heart and lean not on your own understanding. In all your ways acknowledge Him and He will direct your steps."
Proverbs 3:5, 6

Queen for a Day - April 1, 2006

Sister Frances

I'm not sure why you have picked up this book and have read this far. Maybe you are a friend of Sister Frances and you love reading the stories of people just like you or maybe you're a family member reading to discover how many lives Frances touched. Either way, keep reading and allow these stories to renew your strength and re-kindle your faith. I met Sister Frances about two years ago. I don't know why I've called her Sister Frances from day one but she seems to love it, I think it's our special thing.

I'm a lot younger than Frances, about 56 years to be exact but I've never allowed her age to hinder my respect for her and she has never allowed my age to hinder her affection for me. I often ask myself while driving to Frances' home "what devotion will she share with me today?" or "I wonder if she has any chocolate out?" Our times together have been filled with laughter, excitement, prayer and even tears. I would sit in the Jesus chair every time I visited. To be honest I've never felt anything mystical or even spiritual about the chair but I did receive some very spiritual guidance and wisdom while seated there. I can remember my first appointment with her. I had heard much about the chair and I was a bit nervous. I had heard stories of people actually feeling Jesus knees while sitting there. So I sat down and I didn't feel the knobby knees of Christ but what I did experience in that chair was love and affection.

Sister Frances shared with me about the time she died and what she learned from that experience. We would talk about her late hus-band and his love for the church and softball. We would talk about her children and their wonderful families. After a few minutes of chitchat we would get down to business. She would read and I would listen. She would ask a tough question or two and I would answer the best I could. Then she'd say, "Well what do you have for me?" There was always an exchange; she was never interested in just what she could give but what we could give to each other. I think of Psalm 145:4 when I think about our moments together: One generation will commend your works to another; they will tell of your mighty acts. And that's what we did, we bragged on God and then we prayed. I would often leave the Jesus chair and sit at Frances' feet for prayer. We prayed for one another and that was the culmination of our time together.

The Jesus chair was a place of refreshing for me and I would often leave wondering to myself "What would it take to have that kind of fire at that age?" Frances is a true example of a Godly woman and I'm so happy to be a part of her life and to be her student in the wisdom of God.

Blessings!
Dave Simiele

Granny Cummings

The Red Chair

Frances was persistent and persuasive in her requests for me to visit her home and sit a spell in her red chair to share Jesus together. As we swapped our stories of His Story in our lives, the common bond and connection of our sprits to a God who is spirit came into focus. Our time together has been bright with light that He shines on us when we seek Him and share His life together.

I asked Frances how she has learned to live a life in which her spirit is in control as it connects to God, rather than controlled by her body or soul (mind, will and emotions). She described a life process in which distractions have been progressively stripped away, leaving her time and a focus on Jesus that is now allowing her to experience the "time of her life," as she connects with a wide variety of people, many of whom come to sit in her red chair.

We often fail to enjoy God's company, yet we were created to be dissatisfied and incomplete with less. Her aging process with reduced health and family responsibilities parallels my own, with my loss of leg strength from MS, so that we have both begun to find time and to enjoy the presence of God, as never before. I've found few people that share this continuous sense of His presence, a fairly recent experience for me. I find it deeply nourishing to hear the perspective of Frances, who has experienced it for many years.

In particular, I've profited from hearing her describe that the "secret" to be able to continuously hear from God is a continuous dialogue with Him. This means not only prayer and Bible reading, but also time in silence. Just as God spoke to the boy Samuel, David, and Jesus as they spent attentive, silent time during the night hours, so I've heard God tell me to quit praying, to "shut up and listen" to Him. When our hearts are pure and the noise of life has died down, we can actually hear God, who is a spirit. But we can only hear Him in **our spirits,** not with our soul or ears. God is not mute and we must never mistake our deafness for His silence.

We are also adventuring from things we share in our common life in the Spirit of God to those in which our understanding differs, including our views of how the church should function. This exercise is helping us understand that relationship should never be at risk as we work through differences. But we wouldn't begin the adventure if we hadn't first built a relationship that is not at risk, as we explore other dimensions of our life together.

As we grow in our appreciation for the life that God has planted in one another, it seems that we wish others to participate in it. Frances has now asked me to accompany her to meet with her niece by marriage, Aimee, who shares some of the handicaps that MS often brings.

We'll see where the journey takes us. There is no hurry for those of us who have begun an eternal life with God. It seems that the only hurry is to touch the lives of those who don't yet know our lovely Lord Jesus.

Respectfully, your servant in Christ,
Wendell Globig

Brenda, Frances, Beth, Beverly, and Bonita

Comfort

I had been invited to sit in the Jesus Chair many times before finally accepting. It had been about 8 months since my son Mathew had died. My heart was truly broken as Mathew was the love of a lifetime and my best bud. I was so angry that God allowed him to be taken at such an early age. I felt betrayed and forgotten.

I am so thankful for Miss Frances and her "Jesus Chair." She has a level of spiritual wisdom second to few. When she told me that I was a "king's child" it touched the hurt that was locked in the hidden regions of my heart. I love this woman for so many reasons. She reached out and felt my pain. Then she imparted great knowledge of the Bible and was able to apply it to my world. I especially love the way her gentle soft southern voice can sooth you one moment and in the next can raise up, and with what I can only describe as divine empowerment demand you "put on the armor and fight."

It's hard to explain the feeling of sitting in the Jesus Chair for the first time. I can't say that I felt an immediate heavenly presence. What I can say is that I felt an overwhelming sense of comfort. I liken it to the comfort I remember as a small child. If on occasion I had a cut and ran to my mom, she would scoop me up and hold me tight until the hurt disappeared. It is this comfort that seeps slowly from the fabric of the chair and into your waiting heart. It is the comfort of our Father in heaven and it is as a result of Jesus, who is seated beside him, interceding on our behalf. There is a spiritual warmth that it brings to all who seek it.

It's a chair…just like any other, but it is a vehicle for his love and grace.

Miss Frances and her Jesus Chair will forever be near to my heart.

Keith Frank

My Cheerleader

When I think of my Mother, one word that comes to mind is cheerleader. All my life I have been the recipient of her cheering and encouraging me in all my endeavors.

The earliest recollection was when I was 5 years old and started taking piano lessons. Not only was my Mother there to encourage me, she also started taking lessons with me. Her lessons lasted only 1 year, but that was long enough to participate in our first recital. There were lots of students and we all wore formal attire. I'm sure her believing in me was what encouraged me to continue those lessons for 13 years, and according to her, she never had to make me practice.

Throughout all my school years she continued her role as cheerleader. She always seemed so proud of everything I attempted or was a part of; whether it was sports, music, academic accomplishments, friendships or dating. In fact, when Bob and I met and started dating as juniors in high school, she and my entire family joined forces with Bob's family to become a huge cheering squad. It was incredible how much they believed in us!

However, the biggest impact on my life came as she set the example to go after God with all your heart. As the years have gone by, and life has been filled with uncertainties, and, at times, the unexpected, that one constant has always remained— knowing that God is always faithful and His mercies are new every morning.

Thank you, Mama, for your encouragement and example.

Brenda

Make a Difference in Someone's Life

Dear Frances,

In about mid August after I started taking your class "The Bush is Still Burning: The Christ who Makes Things Happen in our Deepest Needs," I started thinking about the expression, "make a difference in someone's life." As I was thinking about a new career, I thought "Lord, I'd like to do something that would make a difference." I began to think about others who had made a difference in my life and that's where you came into the picture. You made a difference in my life!!!

You were the person who talked about getting up early each morning and reading your Bible and praying. I was a new Christian. I decided at that moment that I was going to do that. And what a difference that has made in my life and in my growth. It was a discipline that I looked forward to each morning. What a joy!

Secondly, you suggested that we find a prayer partner. When you said that, Sharion turned around, looked at me and asked, "Do you want to be prayer partners?" And I immediately responded, "Yes." That moment was the beginning of one of the greatest blessings in my life. Sharion and I began to pray for our families, our friends, our work, our church, our pastors and everything the Lord lay on our hearts. We prayed about the difficult things we were going through, and we shared our dreams and deepest desires. The Holy Spirit knit our hearts together in a friendship like none I've ever had before. Our friendship has been a place of safety for me, because I can tell her things and not fear rejection or criticism from her. Next to Jesus, Sharion is my very best friend.

Through being prayer partners we learned how different we are from one another and yet in some ways we are the same. We both love the Lord deeply. We love our children and want for them to follow the Lord wholeheartedly, as we also try to do. But we are very different in our personalities, in our work, and in other ways. What we have in common is — we both love Jesus and we want His perfect will for our lives above all else. Frances, the ironic thing about this friendship is that we were in the same care group together and we were never really close until after we became prayer partners. It was like I knew *of* her, but didn't really *know* her.

Frances, you have made a difference in my life. These two changes in my life have been significant and profound. Recently it occurred to me that because my daily quiet time had changed me, it has also had a rippling effect — you have made a difference in my children's lives! Thank you so much.

*****

Frances, many times I've heard you say you were not an educated woman. I heard Joyce Meyer say the same thing about herself and she gave the scripture verse 1Corinthians 1:26-31: "For you see your calling brethren, that not many wise according to the flesh, not many mighty, not many noble are called. But God has chosen the foolish things of the world to put to shame the wise (Foolish Frances, *my* thoughts!). And God has chosen the weak things of the world to shame the things which are mighty...that no flesh should glory in His Presence..."He who glories, let him glory in the Lord."

Frances, did it ever occur to you that if you had been so highly educated, then you might have been too smart for God to use you? You might have been prideful about your education. As it was, God knew who you were and He chose you, Frances, and you have become a vessel of honor. He knew He could trust you so He gave you a powerful and anointed ministry.

Love,
Susan Hogg

The Jesus Chair & What It Has Meant to Me!

In Matthew 28:19 Jesus told the disciples to go and make disciples of all nations. That means many things to many Christians. Some Christians are called to go to far away countries to reach the lost. Some people go into the city to reach the downtrodden. Some Christians go to the market place and reach businessmen.

Ms. Frances brings thousands of people into her living room to sit in the Jesus Chair. I have sat in that chair a few nights and had Ms. Frances ask me the same question: "What is Jesus doing in your life now?"

One night I told Ms. Frances that I was frustrated and wasn't sure. Sometimes the Bible seems too complicated and maybe I need to go to a better Bible study.

Then she asked me the most important question I ever heard: "What are you doing with what you already know?" "Ouch!" She then poked me with her joystick and told me to go to Philippians 4:4-7

"Rejoice in the Lord always and again I say: Rejoice! Let your gentleness be evident to all. The Lord is near. Do not be anxious about anything, but in everything, by prayer and petition, with thanksgiving, present your requests to God. And the peace of God, which transcends all understanding, will guard your hearts and your minds in Christ Jesus."

What a powerful scripture!

I need to stop by and have Ms. Frances poke me with her joystick in the Jesus Chair again. I really miss my spiritual Momma and having her call me her "little boy!"

Jake Sheaffer

Blessed

Dear Mama,

On this Mother's Day, May 9, 1999 I pause and take time to think back over the last 53 plus years and especially the first nineteen spent in our home — my home; a home full of Jesus and His lessons and examples to me of real love through you, my Mother, who always so intensely and radically loved my Lord and filled our home with that love. Thank you for your always unconditional love; the many dresses you made for me (even when I was carrying my first child), the many times you curled my hair, and always your patience with me when I would turn on all the lights when I was so afraid. Most of all, thank you for introducing me to Jesus and instilling in me a real love for His Word, and for that awesome "prophetic" word over me concerning my future husband! Truly I am blessed of all children (except my four siblings), to have a Mama like you.

I love you.
Beverly Ann

Five Blake Women with Hats

A Different Path

To you who are reading this book, you're getting a small glimpse of what a true Godly woman looks like. I was one of her children who probably made her relationship with the Heavenly Father a much sweeter one. I chose to walk a different path for over half of my life. As we get older (and I am now going on 52) we can only look back and maybe wish we had made better choices. In my case, I feel it was those choices that made me who I am today, which is why my Mom and I are so connected. My God, my Mom, and I share one identical body part — our heart.

As I have read through bits and pieces of some of her journaling, it became quite evident that her number one love, outside of her love for God, was her family. As I stay on my knees for my family, I know my Mom did that so long for me, in her waiting for me to "come home." I thank God every day for the Mom He chose for me.

Bonita Tyree

Bonita, Brenda, Byron, Beverly, and Beth

God Spared Her Life for Me

Frances came into my life twenty years ago. I was a young Mother and wife. I sat in a Sunday school class that met in a home close to the Mechanicsville Christian Center that was taught by Frances twenty years ago. She taught a group of young women to dare to believe in Christ and His endless possibilities for our lives. Christ changed lives and families of those women that attended her class. This was just the beginning of many teaching sessions held by Frances. My faith soared and I experienced God in a very personal and special way in my life and he became physically real to me through her guidance.

God thought I was special enough to spare Frances' life just for me because even after twenty years he knew I needed her guidance and encouragement yet once again. Only eternity will reveal the impact that Frances has had on the lives of the folks that she knew and the folks that she did not know but prayed for. My husband came to know Christ through Frances and he also was filled with the Holy Spirit through her counsel. She taught me how to allow Christ to shine in my life to reach my husband.

I may not have had the pleasure to physically sit in her Jesus chair because distance prevents that but I am there with each telephone conversation we still have.

God only waits for a willing vessel through which his love and wisdom can flow and I thank him daily that Frances has been the vessel that he has chosen to use for me. There is nothing that He will not do to try to reach us.

Frances is and always will be my spiritual Mother. May God bless and keep her in His protection and care always.

Linda Nelson

Seeking Forgiveness

I found myself sitting in the Jesus Chair and while mom was talking to me I was not listening to her as much as I was looking around the room at family pictures she had hanging on the walls. I remembered what my life had been like from a small boy to where I now am in life. I was troubled because no matter what I had done in my life I really wasn't a great success at anything.

I had been married and divorced and had a son named Grayson, the greatest son a man could ever dream of having. I had made up my mind that I would never marry again, and if by some strange event I did remarry, I would never marry a woman with children of her own. Well, you know how God works, especially when you have a praying Mom. I not only remarried, I married a woman that had three children of her own. Now the Lord has blessed us with another son who is fifteen months old and we are expecting our sixth child, a little girl, in September.

Sitting in the Jesus Chair I found myself looking at pictures of my father and thinking what a great man he was—a man of God and high Christ-like morals. My parents were a team. They prayed blessings over each of us, everyday of our lives. My father always praised me for the talents that God had blessed me with, "If I had the talents you do, Son, I would be a millionaire." That made me think, "If I was so talented, then why was I still struggling through life?" Most of my life I had professed to be a Christian, but I still had issues and problems. So here I am in the Jesus Chair, and probably for the first time I could hear Jesus speak to me.

I began to see that I couldn't be successful or feel the blessings that God had in store for me because I was carrying a burden that would not let God's blessings in. It was the same burden that I had been carrying my entire adult life. With every step I took to get away from God, the burden just kept getting bigger and heavier. I finally realized that to receive all of God's blessings I needed to deal with this burden.

For thirty years I had spent my life not being honest with people and doing things that caused pain, anger and distrust in other's lives. I now realized that I needed to humble myself and go back to each and every one of these people and ask them for their forgiveness. I have made a long list of people who in my past I have done an injustice to. With each one, when I go back to ask forgiveness, God blesses me by lifting a small piece of that burden off of me and allowing me to feel His forgiveness. This is a long story. I tell it to you so you can realize it is never too late. I am fifty-four years old and I have been blessed to have a mother who has prayed for me 19,710 days — an intercessor who has kept God holding onto my heart and soul in a way that I could never get away. This woman is Frances Blake, my mother, and this is from her son, Byron.

Byron Blake

Byron and Frances

146

For Frances, Love Connie

I am amazed at the elegant and intricate tapestry that God weaves of our lives. When I decided to help with the youth group at Mechanicsville Christian Center, I had no idea how it would change my life, and how those choices and relationships would still affect me and those I love.

Pastor Carter insisted that everyone on his leadership team be in a discipleship group. He asked Frances to lead the group for the girls. There were three of us and we met weekly. It was a wonderful time of growth. The assignments that Frances gave were meant to "stretch" us and draw us closer to God. I'm sure Carter was hoping they would make us better leaders. I had grown up in the church and had a strong spiritual heritage in my family, but I had never had anyone challenge me in living an authentic faith the way that Frances did—and still does. I still remember some of her assignments, but it was our relationship that was life changing.

When I look back through my journals I see "Frances always says: 'Remember who God is and who you are in Christ…You only have one life to live…live it to the fullest for Jesus Christ…The church has to get back to table fellowship.'"

When I think about Frances the words that come to my mind first are: teachable and selfless. She is always excited about the new things God is teaching her, and amazed that God is using her. I remember how she loved preparing and teaching her ladies Bible study each week. But I never knew her to be downcast or sad when she gave that up to be with her dear Cleveland. She saw each day as a moment of ministry even if it was to be at home to minister quietly to Cleveland or in prayer. People often talk about ministries they used to be involved in, but Frances always thinks she is right now in the best ministry of her life. She is happy to be where God has put her, and she is making "her circumstances work for her."

Even though I live far away now, God is still using her to minister to me. She always calls at just the right time. Her obedience and sensitivity to the Spirit is evident. When we talk on the phone I take notes because I don't want to miss a single pearl of wisdom. Many times in my married life, while my husband and I are dealing with a situation or emotion, Greg will stop, look at me and say, "I love Frances Blake!" He sees the fruit of what she has sown in my life and I realize what a great influence she has had on me.

I have so much to learn to be more like Jesus, and Frances is my example still. Some of my friends haven't had a "Frances," and I feel sorry for them. They haven't sat at the feet of a spiritual mentor, and had a deep relationship with one who will tell you "like it is." So I am trying to be a real and practical friend to those around me. More than anything, I want to always have a teachable spirit, and I want my children to see me continually growing in the faith.

You never know how your actions are going to affect those around you, but when Carter put me in Frances' life I decided that I was never leaving.

Connie Sutherland

My Mother

As you read through the pages of this book, you will get but a small glimpse of a BIG God who is able to do above what we could ever ask or imagine. This is the God my mother loved and served all of my 43 years on this earth thus far. This is the God my mother showed me through her love and example, the God that has never failed to meet every need my mother has had as a happily married woman of 60 years, and as a widow of 7 years.

As long as I've known my mother, there have been three things in her life that I would call her "passions." One — her sewing and knitting. My mother's hands have sewn a many a stitch — not for herself but for so many others. In my home alone, I have two quilts, three afghans, seven cross-stitch pictures, five cross-stitch Christmas stockings, and three old-English prints. Each piece so beautifully and delicately done. Something of my mother's own hand adorns each room in my home.

Another passion is baseball; specifically, the Atlanta Braves baseball team. She is an Atlanta fan and will stayup till 1 a.m. to finish watching a game—especially if it's close or if it's a championship game. I have many memories of being at the baseball field either watching my brother play or cheering the church softball team on while my Daddy coached.

Lastly, her passion for the Lord and His people outweigh them all. She has a passion to see people saved and living the abundant life that the Lord promises us in His Word. Whether it is a Methodist pastor or the appliance repair man, she will talk to you about her Lord and what He is able to do and lead you in the sinner's prayer if needed.

I love my mother and the heritage and foundation of the Lord she has helped instill in my life which is now being instilled in my children's lives. This book is a part of that heritage. The testimonies in this book will be shared with my children and their children and their children's children. God is truly faithful. My mother is a living example of that. Be blessed as you turn the pages of this book. GOD IS FAITHFUL!

Beth Mitten
April, 2007

With Timothy and His Kitten

My Sister Frances

On July 30, 2002 I flew to Virginia to spend the upcoming year with my sister, Frances. Our year together held many special memories; in particular, my 70th birthday when we drove to Smithfield, Virgina and met my dear friend Jinx Parker. It was an exciting day! It has been said that "Just as a shell holds the echo of the sea, the heart holds its memories and its dreams." My seventy years have definitely held many memories and dreams.

Each morning Frances and I studied God's Word, read a devotional book and a Christian novel. Three books — *A Bend in the Road* by David Jeremiah, *My Heart's Cry* by Anne Graham-Lotz, and *The Purpose Driven Life* By Rick Warren — were rich in content. June 13th from *My Utmost for His Highest* by Oswald Chambers left an impression on me — "Never make a principle out of your experiences. Let God be as original with others as He is with you."

As well as reading and studying, both of us enjoy stitchery and knitting projects and listening to Gaither tapes.

I had been with Frances while individuals sat in the red chair and I saw and felt a change in their lives. In January, 2003, having been a Christian since youth, I rededicated my life and made a new commitment to my Lord and Savior. Frances played a vivid part in my growth and commitment and I thank and praise God for our time together.

When you are ready to enlarge your territory, the Spirit of God will increase the power flow within you. You'll know you are working in the realm of a Power greater than yourself, and though you'll be changed by that kind of experience, you will need to stay connected to the Source of Power, the Holy Spirit, to continue to get results.

Little did Frances and I know that the inconveniences of today could and would build character for tomorrow. This leaves me very appreciative of our year spent together. Isn't God great!

Betty J. Greenough

Author's note: It was due to a physical disability that Betty had chosen to spend this time with her sister Frances. Her daughter, Martha, who she depended on for help was facing back surgery and Betty wanted to lighten her load. God works in such mysterious ways!

Frances and Betty

152

Born Again, Again

I felt very close to God this particular week. Spring was here, and as I walked around our farm, I enjoyed His creatures—the birds building their nests, a little goat that I had rescued was now safe, and all our animals seemed content. I began thinking about my life — good as it was — I felt that I was not growing in the Lord enough. I had lost the excitement, the freshness, the joy. I wanted more of Him — I needed more of Him!

Kenny Simpson was holding a class on the Baptism of the Holy Spirit that afternoon. My friend and I made a last minute decision to go. The class was wonderful and I left feeling closer to my Lord but not totally focused on Him. I knew in my heart that I had not surrendered all.

The next day I had questions about the Baptism, so I took them to Frances. She was the first person I met at MCC. I attended a Care Group in her home as a new Christian and I always felt very comfortable asking Frances anything. My questions, of course, were answered, but she didn't stop there. Her spirit knew something was troubling me, so as I sat in "The Jesus Chair" I revealed the hurt in my heart — how the church had treated me during the passing of my father. I didn't feel taken care of in my time of need and I said some things about the church and the leadership to others. Frances said that I had every right to be upset with the church but, according to God's word, I should not have taken my hurt anywhere but to the leadership. So before I left her house, she had me on my knees repenting and asking God's forgiveness. Frances said, "Now you need to go to Carter and ask forgive-ness for what you've spoken" and she gave me Ephesians 4:29-32 to read.

"Speak life, child, not death — let the words out of your mouth edify, build up, strengthen and restore — don't let your words destroy, kill, steal, or take away."

The next day Frances called to ask if I had made that appointment — I told her that I would have Carter and Walter down for lunch and then I'd talk to him, but I couldn't do it this week, maybe next. Frances said, "Linda, don't put it off — you need to do it, child — make that appointment and have them over for lunch later." So I called the church and the secretary proceeded to tell me how booked up Carter was. Then suddenly she discovered an open appointment — saved just for me by God! I called Frances and she said, "Wonderful! Call me before you go, and we'll pray!"

As I prepared to go I received a phone call from France Moore with a "Word," that God had given to her for me. She said that I was not really upset with the Church — I was upset because I lost my father and I missed him! Being angry with the church kept me from focusing on my real hurt — my grief. I was still grieving and I didn't realize it. Her word revealed truth to me and I began to heal.

The day for talking to Carter arrived. Covered in prayer and forgiven by God, I went with excitement and joy in my heart. I asked for forgiveness for all I had said to others about MCC and our leadership. Carter forgave me and he also asked forgiveness. When my dad passed away I saw a need at MCC to prepare meals for members who had lost loved ones, but I was so filled with hurt and anger that I wouldn't listen to God's voice. For many years I had asked God "What can I do for You?" and when He answered me I ignored Him. It was in The Jesus Chair that God gave birth to His new ministry — Congregational Care Ministry (CCM — MCC backwards). I am now working in this ministry with my new friend, France Moore.

Do you remember that I said my walk with the Lord had lost its freshness and excitement? Well, it's back more abundantly. I told Pastor Carter how brand-new I felt. "It sounds like you've been born-again, again." When burdens are lifted and forgiveness is received how renewed and fresh we feel. God blesses me each time I deliver a meal. I am His disciple: I now speak life, not death; I try to walk in

the Spirit, not in the flesh; I try to stay in His Word, and each day I want to do something that has eternal value. It is my honor and privilege to serve the people of MCC, for when I'm serving them, I am serving our wonderful Lord Jesus! We stand ready to serve on His behalf.

> *Therefore, as we have opportunity, let us do good to all people, especially to those who belong to the family of believers.*
> (Galatians 6:10)

Linda Wooddy

You Gave Me Hope

Dear Ms. Frances,

How do I possibly thank you for opening your heart to me? I came to you during a period in my life when I was quite broken, lost and confused. I dreaded opening up to you because I didn't want you to condemn me...even though I condemned myself for all the poor choices and bad decisions I had made up to that point. Yet, as I sat there for the first time in the "Jesus Chair", I saw only warmth and acceptance in your eyes.

You spoke truth, and you didn't sugar coat it. You told me to "walk in the truth that I already knew" and to remember that I was a Princess, the daughter of a King. You also let me know that I would indeed have to reap what I sowed...but you pointed out to me that God's blessings could and would override my reaping. You gave me hope by pointing out that our God is above all else a loving and merciful God. You allowed me to come and pour out my heart week after week as God spoke to me through you and slowly my wounds began to heal.

What an odd pair we made — on the surface at least. You with your silver hair, me with dread locs; you with the regal carriage, me the awkward colt. We came from different backgrounds, different life experiences, but our love for Jesus brought us together. And every single time God showed up and was right there in the middle of us. We both felt His presence and His power...and His love.

Your life is an awesome testimony to the unconditional love of Jesus. You give so freely of yourself: your time, your wisdom, your gifts. I believe God speaks to you and through you in powerful ways, and it is my privilege, my joy and my pleasure to spend time with you. Thank you so much for walking through a dark time with me

and helping me to walk out on the other side. I pray that God uses my life as He uses yours — for His honor and His glory and to help other hurting souls find their way.

All my love and gratitude,
Charlotte Flowers

Catherine, Granny, Betty, Frances - Frances' sisters and mother

BEAUTIFUL REMNANTS
SEWN INTO HER LIFE

The following entries have meant very much to Frances but they did not fit into the design of the earlier chapters. So I have pieced them together here for you to enjoy. They shed more light on the workings of the Lord in Frances' life. They are like the newspaper clippings, the prayers, the photos, or special letters tucked into a mother's Bible, mementos held dear to her heart.

A Vessel to Use

The Master was searching for a vessel to use. On the shelf there were many, which one would He choose? "Take me," cried the gold one, "I'm shiny and bright. My beauty and luster will outshine the rest, for someone like You, Master, I will be best."

The Master passed on with no word at all, and looked at a silver urn, narrow and tall. "I'll serve You, dear Master, I'll pour out Your vine. I'll be at Your table whenever You dine." My lines are so graceful, and my carving so true, and silver would always compliment You."

Unheeding , the Master passed on to the brass . It was wide mouthed and shallow and polished like glass. "Here, here!" cried this vessel, "I know I will do. Place me at Your table for all men to view."

"Look at me !" cried the goblet of crystal so clear. "My transparency shows my contents so dear. Though fragile am I, I will serve You with pride, and I would be happy in Your house to abide."

The Master came next to a vessel of wood. Polished and carved, it solidly stood. "You may use me, dear Master," the wooden bowl said, "but I'd rather You use me for fruit...please, no bread."

The Master looked down and saw this vessel of clay. Empty and broken, it helplessly lay. No hope had this vessel the Master might choose, to cleanse and make whole, to fill, and to use. "Ah," He said, "This is the vessel I've been hoping to find. I will mend it, and cleanse it, I'll make it all mine. I need not the vessel with pride of itself, not the one so narrow that sits on the shelf, or the one who is big mouthed, shallow, and loud, nor the one who displays their contents so proud. Not the one who thinks he can do all things just right, but this plain earthen vessel filled with my power and might." Then gently He lifted the vessel of clay. He mended and cleansed it, and filled it that day. He spoke to it kindly, "There's work you must do. You pour out to others, and I'll pour into you."

Author unknown

In a phone conversation in 2003 Frances told her good friend Shirley Butler that God was calling her to give up her rights — especially her rights to her "self". Shirley responded shortly afterwards with this letter and teaching to encourage her friend.

My Dearest Frances,
    I was so blessed to have the brief time with you on the phone.

God always pours forth a word for me. It always builds up my Spirit man and sends me forward. Thank you, precious one, for your love and dedication to the Father, His Son, and the Sweet Holy Spirit.

As we talked I tossed out the Message of the Giants that represent Spirits of the Enemy that war against us today. Truth of the whole thing is: They are defeated! Their only power is what we are willing to give them! Praise the Lord!

I jotted down some core facts for you. There is so much to learn about each one and the tactics he uses (which are lying spirits) to defeat the Body of Christ. Henry preached a full five-day revival on this topic to the Glory of God. It came forth in the anointing of the Holy Spirit, with no notes or tapes. So God meant it to be an ongoing message. And believe me it is.

Self is our biggest challenge. His intent is to redevelop the UN-HOLY TRINITY'S kingdom of "ME, MYSELF AND I." As the Lord gives me time and unction, I'll share more.

With a more perfect heart each day,

I love you,
Shirley

Five Giants

The story of David is often cut short. We get excited about the giant Goliath being taken down and forget the rest of the story as it's played out. The fact is…David chose 5 smooth stones from the brook put them in his shepherd's bag, and his sling was in his hand. Only one stone was used on Goliath. Our weapons for warfare need to be as prepared and ready as David's were.

This Philistine giant, Goliath, is the first picture of the enemy's warfare. His name means "denuder" or "stripper," one who tries to

161

rob you of your identity. The first thing he said to David was "Who do you think you are?" Believe me, David knew his true identity. He didn't give Goliath his human pedigree. He said, "I come to you in the name of the Lord of Hosts, the God of the armies of Israel, whom you have defiled."

Goliath vs. David: Goliath called himself "champion". David was the Anointed One. A champion was a middleman who could decide the outcome with one single-handed fight. The real enemy had sold this giant a lie. He didn't know his own identity. David knew the truth about who he was! David was the real champion who would decide the outcome of this battle. He had proven his weapons and had single handedly destroyed every enemy that had come out against him and his flock.

Personal application: Are my weapons of warfare proven and ready to use: The enemy will surely come to try to rob us of our identity. "Are you really a Christian? God doesn't care about you, Miss Goody Two Shoes." I know immediately that my feet shod with the preparation of the Gospel of Peace have scared him silly. He wants me to believe that they are just "goody two shoes," but I know the truth. Our armor terrifies the enemy.

There's no record of how David used the last four stones, but there is a record of whom they were meant for and who took down those last four giants.

2 Samuel 21:15-22 David grows faint and is taken out of the battle. The second giant, Ishbi-Benob, whose name means "discourager," comes out with a new sword and thinks he can kill David. Abishai, whose name means "faithfulness of God," comes to David's aid and kills this second giant.

The third giant, Saph, whose name means "the destroyer," comes out in another battle at Gob. Sibbechai, whose name means "divine intervention" (God will supernaturally entwine Himself around you), killed this giant.

The fourth giant LaHmi (1 Chronicles 20:5), whose name means "harasser," is the brother of Goliath. He comes to war again at Gob. Now that the destroyer is taken out, the only weapon left is for this character to harass, aggravate, or intimidate, to what he hopes will be death. Elhanan, whose name means "the mercy of God" or "the shelter of grace," kills this giant.

Now, there is only one more giant left to contend with. Verse 20 describes him as another man of great stature." He boasts of six fingers on each hand and six toes on each foot. He is SELF PLEAS-ING, proud, arrogant, and boastful. All the attributes of the other giants are rolled into this one, but without power. 3John 9 gives us a name for such a one as this. Diotrephes, "one who loves to have preeminence among them, does not receive us." He is a self-seeker, God unto himself, the opposite of submission, rather a manipulator, controller. John says he wrote a letter to this church, but there's no record of it. It's believed that Diotrephes possibly destroyed it. This enemy doesn't want to be exposed to the real truth. Jonathan, whose name means "Truth given by God," kills this last giant of self.

How does this speak to us personally, about our encounters with these same spirits that have come out against us today? The enemy is such a dummy; he keeps playing the same tricks, and wearing the same disguises.

Excerpts from another letter from Shirley Butler written in December 2001 reflecting on the Christmas season and what was happening in Frances' life as Cleveland was preparing to enter Heaven's gates:

My Dear Frances,

The Lord has given you many names to be identified with. I've never called you Mrs. Blake, for from the very first meeting you

have been a Spiritual Mother from God to my life. Is it any wonder that as we talked on the phone on December 15, the Lord gave me a new way to identify you. You said to me, "Shirley, the Glory of God is so awesome. There is so much JOY!" You said, "I am so thankful to be alive at this time, to see how the Glory of the Lord is being revealed." As we talked about how God is truly disclosing Himself to us in these days, I heard the Lord say to me…

"My daughter, Frances, is the Living Nativity!"

Frances, I was reminded of the times in our previous churches when Henry and I had invited people to stand in a little shed on the church lawn and *PRETEND* for a brief period of time that they were the *LIVE NATIVITY*. How futile are our attempts to capture that HOLY MOMENT. Yet—a Living Nativity—is exactly how the Lord identified you to me in our conversation.

When you asked me to help you to understand just what I meant, I began to ponder in my heart and listen to the Lord for more understanding. I also found Webster's dictionary to say: Nativity is the process of being born! Is that exciting??? Having had the privilege to be in the birthing suite when most of my grandchildren (were born) I can tell you there was exuberant JOY!!! There were tears and laughter, and sometimes pain and sorrow. It is with those same emotions that I write to you. What a joy to remember the day I was Born of the Spirit in the kitchen of your home and then two weeks later my precious Henry was Born Again in your den.…

Frances, the fact is…each time we share I come with a spirit of expectation, pregnant and ready to give birth to a new thing from God. For I know that He is always preparing something special in and through you! Frances, you have prepared your life to be the birthing suite…Most of these babies arrive in this birthing suite like Henry and I did, *bloody and bruised from the journey.* You have already planned for that! The washing begins with the water of God's Word. Little babies need to be fed often and their diet has to change

and increase as they grow into maturity. My, how you have fed us! ...We know (you) will have a nutritious meal prepared. For you continually gather and keep your SPIRITUAL PANTRY well stocked with GOOD THINGS so that no one goes away hungry.

Now we know that a washed clean, well-fed baby is a HAPPY BABY! Frances, we babies who leave your breast, leave with more than just a temporary happy moment meal. We carry away the JOY OF THE LORD, which is our strength to carry on throughout eternity. This same JOY overflows through the generations to follow.

It is A Heavenly Legacy that begins with a Living Nativity!

Thank you, Frances, for being a Living Nativity in my life! I love you!

Shirley

Another excerpt from Shirley's journal reflecting on the Christmas Story and Cleveland's funeral:

Is it any wonder that, on that December day in the year of 2000 as Henry and I drove to the funeral home, God spoke these words to my heart: "YOU SHALL FIND THE BABE WRAPPED IN SWADDLING CLOTHES, LYING IN A MANGER."

Frankly, I was a bit puzzled. As I pictured the scene in my mind, I saw the room where Cleveland lay *wrapped in swaddling clothes of death*. All around him the new life, the work of the Holy Spirit...The tears were replaced with joy! The brokenness of this precious man now healed and whole. Little did I know that God would unfold to me the TRUE STORY OF CHRISTMAS!

A place which the world sees as an ending place was in TRUTH, a BIRTHING SUITE! This is not the ending of a wonderful story but THE BEGINNING. For what God birthed afresh in me that day

changed my whole conception of Christmas:…The Blake family had gathered around the earthly remains of our Beloved Cleveland. Usually this is a time of great sadness when Henry and I are praying for wisdom to restore hope to the broken and torn lives of those left behind. Not needed here!

The mood of those gathered here was of Serene Joy! Going to the place where I found Frances, seated on a love seat, I sat down beside her. Hugging her, I asked, "How are you, Frances?" Her reply were words that you expect to hear in the Christmas story. "Shirley, I have PEACE, such PEACE!" The Prince of Peace was truly in residence, reigning in you, Frances. I watched it (peace) flow out of her to each one of the family and friends gathered there. Peace on earth now and good will toward men! The solemn good byes to the earthly part now will give way to the joyful "Hello's". I see Angels announcing the good news! I see shepherds paying respect…The Christmas scene is in my midst...Thanks be to God for the ONE willing to die in our midst to make this happen today. Blessed be the spirit of Cleveland Blake as you now take up your new residence in the Heavenly Realms of Glory.

12/21/00 While all the shoppers in the Christmas rush are out in force, Henry and I gather to pray with expectancy. My devotion read: WE must see beyond the familiar elements of Christmas and realize that at its heart, Christmas is a CELEBRATION OF THE INCARNATION OF GOD as He discloses HIMSELF to us. IN HIS PRESENCE EVERY TRUTH IS REVEALED!

*****

We gather at MCC to worship and thank God for the life of Cleveland:

AN ORDINARY CARPENTER BECOMES EXTRAORDINARY AS THE TRUTH OF HIS LIFE IS REVEALED!

Beverly Anne sang "Because He lives" with the same anointing that Frances has always had…And the music from the piano by Brenda's hands felt like pure Gold as it fell on my ears.

Lord, how did you work all things in my life to bring me back to Richmond for such a time as this? A thousand sermons of Christmas have all been wrapped into ONE LIVE PRODUCTION for this little servant girl's understanding of just HOW AWESOME YOU ARE!!!

Thank you, Lord, and thank you to the Blake Family for being a bright, shining reflection of Christ—My first LIVING NATIVITY.

Shirley Butler

Devotional for Caregivers

Frances' faithfulness to have a daily devotion with the Lord has helped to sustain her through the trials that she has endured in life. One of the most difficult challenges was to care for her husband Cleveland as he slipped into the grip of Alzheimer's. The following thoughts and scriptures taken from <u>Come Home to Hope</u> *by Sharon Hoffman helped to sustain Frances through those sometimes turbulent days and enabled her to find the grace to minister to her ailing husband, her "man," as she liked to call him.*

When I accepted Jesus into my life, I transferred the title and deed over to Jesus. As owner and Master of my heart, Christ has the freedom to manage and operate my life as He chooses. I couldn't live a pleasing Christian life in my own strength. It would be impossible. Giving Him daily control makes sure that I do not take it back.

The gift of salvation is not the last gift God offers us. It's the first of many. It sets the pattern for all that follows. Let's look at all the other gifts He freely bestowed on His children.

167

First of all, I have confidence-the inner confidence that comes from God Himself. "God did not give us a spirit of timidity, but a spirit of power, of love and of self discipline." (2 Timothy 1:17)

I am confident that I am never alone because God has said, "Never will I leave you, never will I forsake you." (Hebrews 13:5)

I am confident that He will always provide for me. "I was young and now I am old, yet I have never seen the righteous forsaken or their children begging bread." (Psalm 37:25)

I am confident that I can make it through whatever life brings my way for "I can do everything through Christ who gives me strength." (Philippians 4:13)

I am confident in my relationship with Christ. "I know whom I have believed, and am convinced that He is able to guard what I have entrusted to Him for that day." (2 Timothy 1:12)

I am confident that I can trust God implicitly to be at work in my life. "My grace is sufficient for you, for my power is made perfect in weakness." (2Corinthians 12:9)

I am confident that I can rely on God, no matter what. "In quietness and trust is your strength." (Isaiah 30:15)

Second gift, I have a calm that I can live in safety and without fear. "Do not fear, for I am with you; do not be dismayed, for I am your God. I will strengthen you and help you, I will uphold you with my righteous right hand." (Isaiah 41:10)

I have a calm during the storms of life for God has promised, "When you pass through the waters, I will be with you; and when you pass through the rivers, they will not sweep over you." (Isaiah. 43:2)

I calmly do not have to be afraid when others attack me. "The Lord is a refuge for the oppressed, a stronghold in times of trouble." (Psalm 9:9)

I can know calm and quiet in this noisy world. "Whoever listens to me will live in safety and be at ease, without fear of harm." (Proverbs 1:33)

I can calmly face the future. "For I know the plans I have for you, declares the Lord, plans to prosper you and not to harm you, plans to give you hope and a future." (Jeremiah 29:11)

I can feel calm when I feel like I'm going to lose my mind! "And the peace of God, which transcends all understanding, will guard your hearts and your minds in Christ Jesus." (Philippians 4:7)

I have an unexplainable calm that nothing in this world can offer, for Jesus said, "Peace I leave with you; my peace I give you. I do not give to you as the world gives. Do not let your hearts be troubled and do not be afraid." (John 14:27)

The third gift is the unlimited comfort available to me. To belong to the Creator of the world, what could be a greater comfort? He knows me and sees me, cares for me and loves me! (Psalm 147)

I have comfort because the Comforter actually lives within my heart. "And I will ask the Father, and he will give you another Counselor to be with you forever- the Spirit of Truth. The world cannot accept him, because it neither sees Him nor knows Him; but you know Him, for He lives with you and will be in you." (John 14:16-17)

What comfort to know that God is in control. He's omnipotent, having all power. (Luke 1:35); omnipresent, everywhere present at the same time (Psalm 139:7); and omniscient, all knowing. (1 Corinthians 2:10-11)

Comfort is mine when I am brokenhearted. "The sacrifices of God are a broken spirit; a broken and contrite heart, O God, you will not despise." (Psalm 51:17)

My heart is comforted when I realize that I am going to be with Jesus in my heavenly home eternally. "We are confident, I say, and would prefer to be away from the body and at home with the Lord." (2 Corinthians 5:8)

I am comforted in any circumstance when I feel like everything or everyone is against me. "If God is for us, who can be against us?" (Romans 8:31)

I can think of nothing more comforting than realizing God is with me always. "Never will I leave you; never will I forsake you." (Hebrews 13:5)

I find comfort in knowing that God's plan is not for me to fail, but to succeed. "For I know the plans I have for you, declares the Lord, plans to prosper you and not to harm you, plans to give you hope and a future." (Jeremiah 29:11)

Comfort is available during excruciatingly painful and trying times in my life. "And we know that all things God works for the good of those who love Him, who have been called according to His purpose." (Romans 8:28)

I am secure and comforted in accepting the love of Christ. "Who shall separate us from the love of Christ? Shall trouble or hardship or persecution or famine or nakedness or danger or sword? No, in all these things we are more than conquerors through Him who loved us. For I am convinced that neither death, life, angels, demons, present, future, powers, height, depth, nor anything else will be able to separate us from the love of God that is in Christ Jesus our Lord." (Romans 8: 35-39)

Frances: Since August 2, 1998, when God brought me back from death to life, I am more confident than ever that I am never alone. God will never leave me nor forsake me. I know that I can do all things through Christ that strengthens me, and that I can trust God and rely on Him no matter what.

I thank God for all His blessings upon me as He uses Cleveland to teach me such wonderful spiritual truths. The wisdom that the Lord imparts to me is so great that more and more Cleveland is calm and easier to work with. Life is so exciting for me as I see more of God at work throughout the day. Truly I am experiencing a great miracle.

I just want to say that if we could get up every morning expecting and looking for what God is going to do and say to us for this day we will live a life of happiness and joy like we've never known. "This is the day that the Lord hath made. Let us rejoice and be glad in it." (Psalm 118:24)

The following verses brought such healing as it was quickened to my spirit. "Rejoice not against me, O mine enemy; when I fall, I shall arise. (Micah 7:8a) And then another came into my spirit when things seemed to fail. "Yet I will rejoice in the Lord, I will joy in the God of my salvation. The Lord is my strength, and He will make my feet like hind's feet, and he will make me to walk upon high places." (Habakkuk 3:18,19)

The Devil's Convention

Satan called a worldwide convention. In his opening address to his evil angels, he said, "We can't keep the Christians from going to church. We can't keep them from reading their Bibles and know the truth. We can't even keep them from conservative values. But we can do something else. We can keep them from forming an intimate, abiding relationship in Christ. If they gain that connection with Jesus, our power over them is broken. So let them go to church, let them have their conservative lifestyles, but steal their time, so they can't gain that experience in Jesus Christ. This is what I want you to do, Angels. Distract them from gaining old of their Savior and maintaining that vital connection throughout their day!"

"How shall we do this?" shouted his angels.

"Keep them busy in the non-essentials of life and invent un-numbered schemes to occupy their minds," he answered. "Tempt them to spend, spend, spend, then borrow, borrow, borrow. Convince the wives to go to work for long hours and the husbands to work six or seven days a week, 10 12 hours a day, so they can afford their lifestyles. Keep them from spending time with their children. As their family fragments, soon, their homes will offer no escape from the pressure of work."

"Overstimulate their minds so that they cannot hear that still small voice. Entice them to play the radio or cassette player whenever they drive, to keep the TV, VCR, CDs, and their PC's going constantly in their homes. And see to it that every store and restaurant in the world plays non-biblical, contradicting music constantly. This will jam their minds and break that union with Christ."

"Fill their coffee tables with magazines and newspapers. Pound their minds with the news twenty-four hours a day. Invade their driving moments with billboards. Flood their mailboxes with junk mail, sweepstakes, mail-order catalogs, and every kind of newsletter and promotional offering free products, services, and false hopes."

"Even in their recreation, let them be excessive. Have them return from their recreation exhausted, disquieted, and unprepared for the coming week. Don't let them go out in nature to reflect on God's wonders. Send them to amusement parks, porting events, concerts, and movies instead."

"And when they meet for spiritual fellowship, involve them in gossip and small talk so that they leave with troubled consciences and unsettled emotion. Let them be involved in soul winning, but crowd their lives with so many good causes they have not time to seek power from Christ. Soon they will be working in their own strength, sacrificing their health, and family for the good of the cause."

It was quite a convention in the end. And the evil angels went eagerly to their assignment causing Christians everywhere to get busy, busy, busy and rush here and there.

Has the devil been successful at his scheme? You be the judge…

Satan's goal is to take our minds and hearts off Christ then steer us toward the cares of the world. God wants us to enjoy life, but He must be first.

If we are too busy for God, then we are too busy.

Author unknown

172

In preparation to teach a class on Prayer Frances searched the scriptures and read from two of her favorite mentors Watchman Nee and Andrew Murray. The following is a portion of the teaching that she presented at MCC in 2006.

Let Us Examine Ourselves:
Read Psalm 51. (Note Ps. 51:10)

Have mercy upon me, O God,
According to your lovingkindness;
According to the multitude of Your tender mercies,
Blot out my transgressions.
Wash me thoroughly from my iniquity,
And cleanse me from my sin.

For I acknowledge my transgressions,
And my sin is always before me.
Against You, You only, have I sinned,
And done this evil in Your sight—
That You may be found just when You speak,
And blameless when You judge.

Behold, I was brought forth in iniquity,
And in sin my mother conceived me,
Behold, You desire truth in the inward parts,
And in the hidden part You will make me to know wisdom.

Purge me with hyssop, and I shall be clean;
Wash me, and I shall be whiter than snow.
Make me hear joy and gladness,
That the bones You have broken may rejoice.

Hide Your face from my sins,
And blot out all my iniquities.
Create in me a clean heart, O God,
And renew a steadfast spirit within me.
Do not cast me away from Your presence,
And do not take your Holy Spirit from me.

Restore to me the joy of Your salvation,
And uphold me by Your generous Spirit.
Then I will teach transgressors Your ways,
And sinners shall be converted to You.

Deliver me from the guilt of bloodshed, O God,
The God of my salvation.
And my tongue shall sing aloud of Your righteousness.
O Lord, open my lips,
And my mouth shall show forth Your praise.
For You do not desire sacrifice, or else I would give it;
You do not delight in burnt offering.
The sacrifices of god are a broken spirit,
A broken and a contrite heart—
These, O God, You will not despise.

****

Let us have our prayer line up with God's will, that is, His Word.
As we begin to pray let us ask God to:
• Search me, O God, and know my heart; try me, and know
my thoughts;
And see if there be any wicked way in me, and lead me in the
way everlasting. (Psalm 139:23, 24 KJV)
• Pray for cleansing (to free from dirt, defilement, or guilt).

174

Come to God with clean hands (free from impurities, morally pure). Come to God with the right motive.

• Ask God "to teach me to do Thy will; for Thou art my God; Thy spirit is good; lead me into the land of uprightness." (Ps. 143:10)

• Understand that "Not every one that saith unto me, Lord, Lord, shall enter into the Kingdom of heaven; but he that doeth the will of my Father which is in heaven." (Mt. 7:21)

• Understand that "We ought to obey God, rather than man." (Acts 5:29)

• Know that "If ye keep my commandments, ye shall abide in my love." (John 15:10)

• Understand that "Ye are my friends, if ye do whatsoever I command you." (John 15:14)

• "For whosoever shall do the will of my Father which is in heaven; the same is my brother and sister, and mother." (Mt.12:50)

• "Not with eye service, as men pleasers; but as the servants of Christ, doing the will of God from the heart." (Eph. 6:6)

• Mortify your members which are upon the earth; fornication, uncleanness, inordinate affection, evil concupiscence, and covetousness, which is idolatry." (Col. 3:5,Rom. 12:1,2)

• Watch your speech, thoughts and imaginations. (Col 4:6, Eph. 4:29, 11Cor. 10:5)

• If we confess our sins, He is faithful and just to forgive us our sins and to cleanse us from all unrighteousness. (1John 1:9)

Concerning God's Will

When God is working in us to will we must set our faces like a flint to carry out this will, and must respond with an emphatic "I will" to every "Thou shalt" of His. For God can only carry out His own will with us as we consent to it, and (set our) will in harmony with His.

So, Let us submit ourselves to the plain teaching of the Word, such as:
1) The matter of dress (1 Peter 3:3, and 1 Tim. 2:9)
2) The matter of conversation (Eph. 4:29, 5:4)
3) The matter of avenging injuries and standing up for our rights (Ro. 12:19-21, Mt. 5:38-48, 1 Peter 2:19-21)
4) The matter of forgiving one another (Eph. 4:32; Mk 11:25,26)
5) The matter of conformity to the world (Rom.12:2, 1John 2:15-17, James 4:4)
6) The matter of anxieties of every kind (Mt 6:25-34. Phil.4:6,7)

Father, God gives me in the Word what He means for me to be:
1) Completely humble and gentle – patient (Eph.4:2)
2) Strong in the Lord (Eph.6:10)
3) Without complaining or arguing (Phil. 2:14)
4) Not anxious, guarded by peace (Ph.4:6-7)
5) Forgiving, loving (Col. 3:13-14)
6) Encouraging one another (1 Th. 5:11)
7) Respectful of leadership (1 Th. 5:12)
8) Always joyful (1 Th. 5:16)
9) Continually praying (1 Th. 5:17)

Harmonious Will

According to the word in Genesis 2 God gave man a free will when He created him. God has His will, but so too has man his will.

When a man's will is not in agreement with God's will, God is instantly restricted. From the day God created man and even up to this present hour, man's free will may either allow or hinder God's authority to get through. So we can see that during this period of time, between two eternities, the authority of God is restricted by man. In the future eternity, man's free will shall become one with the eternal will of God. There will become perfect harmony between God and man.

Today the church (us) stands on earth for the will of God. If we (the church) are unable to rise up to the will of God, He (God) will be restricted. Although we (the church) possess a free will, we must put it in full subjection to the authority of God.

The church is a group of born-again people who have been redeemed by the precious blood, regenerated by the Holy Spirit, and have committed themselves into God's hands, accepting His will and standing on the earth for Him to maintain His testimony...

Prayer as work means that we stand on God's side, desiring what He desires. To pray according to God's will is a most powerful thing.

Three imposing principles of prayer found in Matt. 18:18-20:

1) What things soever ye shall bind on earth shall be bound in heaven; and what things soever ye shall loose on earth shall be loosed in heaven. (vs.18)....Many are the people and things that are contradictory to Him; and all these God expects to be bound. Many also are these people and things that are spiritual, valuable, profitable, sanctified, and these He anticipates to be loosed. We cannot increase God's power, but we can hinder it. The church is God's chosen vessel wherein is placed the will of God so that she may pronounce on earth God's Will.

2) What is the Prayer Ministry of the church (us)? It is God telling the church what He wishes to do so that the church on earth can then pray it out. How can we (the church) bind and loose as the Word says?

Harmony in the Holy Spirit

We must see that what the Lord is doing... It is not simply an agreeing in the asking of any one thing, rather it is an agreeing on earth as touching everything, whatever we ask. This is the oneness of the body or oneness of the Holy Spirit. If we are not praying in harmony of the Holy Spirit, heaven will not bind or loose. This says that two must be harmonious concerning any and every matter. We are both brought to a place where there is such harmony as is true in music.

We want Your Will to be done—as in heaven, so on earth...

For the sake of His testimony, God must obtain a vessel through which He may do all His works. The church should pray, preparing the Way of God, that the eternal purpose of God will get through.

As we stand in the rightful place in the body — denying our flesh and not asking for ourselves but for the will of God to be done on earth — we shall see how harmonious is prayer. "For where two or three are gathered in my name, there am I in the midst of them."(Matthew 18:20)

Authoritative Prayer

In the Bible can be found a kind of prayer that is the highest and most spiritual. It is authoritative prayer. Matthew 18:18 is an authoritative prayer.

In Exodus 14 we see that Moses cried to the Lord only to hear God say "wherefore criest thou unto me? Speak unto the children of Israel that they go forward. And lift thou up thy rod, and stretch out thy hand over the sea, and divide it, and the children of Israel shall go into the midst of the sea on dry ground." Moses here learned and experienced Authoritative prayer of command.

Ascension

In our day where does prayer of command find its origin with the Christian? It has its origin at the ascension of the Lord. Ascension is very much related to the Christian life. Ascension gives us victory. Just as the death of Christ solves our old creation in Adam, and resurrection leads us into the new creation, so Ascension gives us a new position in the face of Satan.

We see in Ephesians 1:20-22a that as Christ ascends to heaven He opens a way to heaven so then His Church (us) may also ascend from earth to heaven. We know that Satan dwells in the air. This way was formerly blocked by Satan, but now Christ has opened it up. God has caused Satan and all his subordinates to be subject to Christ. He has put all things under His feet. While the death and resurrection is for redemption, ascension is for warfare. Thank God we see in Eph. 2:6 that He has "raised us up with Him, and made us to sit with Him in the heavenly places, in Christ Jesus."

This is the same as telling us that the church is also far above all rule and authority and power and dominion and every name that is named not only in this world, but also in that which is to come.

As all spiritual foes are surpassed by the Lord at His Ascension, so too are these foes surpassed by the church (us) which has ascended with the Lord. In Ephesians 2 we *sit* with Christ, while Ephesians 6 says to *stand*, which signifies we are standing against all principalities, powers, the world-rulers of this darkness, against the spiritual hosts of wickedness in the heavenly places and having done all, to stand.

Ephesians 6:18, 19a is the prayer of spiritual warfare. This kind of prayer is different from the ordinary kind. The ordinary kind is praying from earth to heaven, but the spiritual warfare prayer is a standing in the heavenly position from heaven down to earth. In spiritual warfare this kind of *praying downward* is very important.

What is praying downward? It is standing upon the heavenly position Christ has given us and using authority to resist all the works of Satan by commanding that whatever God has commanded must be done. This is the prayer of command. We are brought into this heavenly position when Christ ascended to heaven. This is the position of victory. All victories are gained by standing in the heavenly, triumphant position. Satan will tempt you, saying "You are on earth." He wants you to be defeated by saying that you are on earth, but you must stand and reply, "As Christ is in heaven, so I am in heaven. I am laying hold of my heavenly position and I am victorious." Authoritative Prayer is based on this heavenly position.

What is Authoritative Prayer?

It is the type of prayer mentioned in Mark 11:23, 24. God does not exhort us to speak to God, He instructs us to speak to the mountain. Authoritative prayer is not asking God to do something but using God's authority to deal directly with the problem. God tells us that we ourselves should speak to the mountain. God has given us the authority as His child to speak to any difficulty and say, "In the name of the Lord Jesus I ask you to leave me or I will not allow you to remain in my life." Before we pray this way, have complete faith, doubt not that what we do is in perfect accord with God's Will. Whatever blocks you in your spiritual course is something you may command to depart from you.

*"Her children rise up
and call her blessed."*
Proverbs 31:28a

Frances and Jeanie Brown